CONTENTS

WORLD WAR I

 Watch out for the *Sign of the Foot*. When ~~~
in the book it means there ~~~
the page. Like here.

DOODLE-BUG AGAIN!

SO WHO WON THE WAR?

WHAT WAS THE POINT
OF IT ALL?

WORLD WAR I

BEFORE IT BEGINS

ALL'S QUIET

Once upon a time there was a mighty continent. Its name was Europe and the year was 1914. It was at peace:

Farmers were free to till the land.

There was work in the factories.

The rich lived comfortably.

Artists painted and musicians played beautiful music.

Scientists discovered new wonders.

Then something horrible happened ...

WAR!

The mighty continent was torn apart by a terrible war. The most terrible war there had ever been - over nine million soldiers died. Before the war these same soldiers had been the farmers, the workers, the scientists and the musicians who had lived peacefully in the mighty continent. After it was over, their bodies, if laid head to toe, would have stretched for 15,084 kilometres (9,375 miles) - nearly half way around the world. A generation of young men was slaughtered.

This terrible war was called the Great War because there'd never been another war like it. Later, after a second terrible war twenty-one years later, the Great War became known as World War I and the new war was called World War II.

WHO, WHEN, WHERE - AND WHY?

WHO:

The war was fought between two groups of countries. On one side were the *Allies* 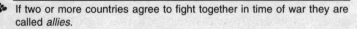, including Britain, France and Russia, and on the other side were the *Central Powers*, including Germany, the Austro-Hungarian Empire and Turkey. Towards the end of the war the USA joined the Allies.

The Allies won and the Central Powers lost.

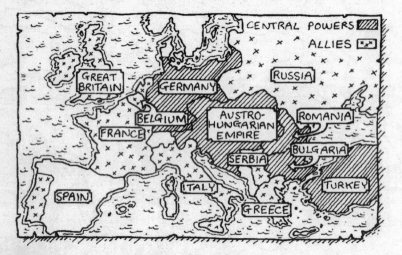

WHEN:

World War I started in the summer of 1914 and finished in November 1918. It had four stages:

1 1914 *'It'll be over by Christmas'*. At this stage most people thought it would be a short war.

2 1915 *'Stuck in the mud'*. Nobody won and nobody lost. Armies got bogged down where they were.

If two or more countries agree to fight together in time of war they are called *allies*.

3 1916-17 *'Slaughter'*. Generals spent the lives of their men by the million trying to clamber out of the mud.

4 1917-18 *'The end game'*. Russia stopped fighting due to a revolution, the USA joined in and tanks were used in battle. The Central Powers crumbled.

WHERE:

Most of the fighting was in Europe, along a line from the English Channel to Switzerland, also in eastern Europe. There was some fighting in the Middle East and Africa as well.

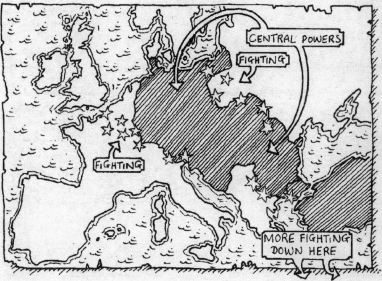

WHY:

In 1914 the rulers of Germany told themselves that Germany was in danger of attack by her neighbours. So they decided to attack first.

Their plan was to win a quick war against France in the west, followed by another quick war against Russia in the east. They seized an excuse and started fighting.

The Germans took a huge risk and it went horribly wrong. The quick war turned into a long slogging match against a more powerful enemy, which, if the truth be told, the Germans never really had much chance of winning.

As they were about to find out ...

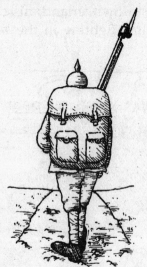

PARADISE LOST

THE WORLD BEFORE THE WAR

Once the war had started, soldiers looked back on the world before the war as if it had been some sort of paradise. That paradise was a more simple place than the world we know today. Before 1914 many of the gadgets and gizmos that we take for granted had been invented but they were too expensive for most people.

THINGS PEOPLE DIDN'T HAVE IN 1914

Aeroplanes (All right, so most people don't own aeroplanes even nowadays, but at least we get to fly in them.)

 Cars

Washing machines

 Fridges

 Radios

Hoovers

Electric lights in houses

Televisions (not invented yet)

Central-heating

THINGS PEOPLE DID HAVE IN 1914

In 1914 there had been no major war in Europe for over forty years. The world was a quieter and more peaceful place than it is today. Life was good and getting better - for the rich and the middle classes anyway.

Even in Britain, then the most industrialised country in the world, the countryside was beautiful with lots of hedges and small fields.

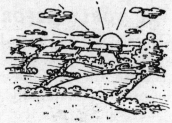

Many people still worked on the land. Gentle winding lanes connected the villages and each village was a world of its own, with its own shops and school.

The pace of life was slower. Cars were rare. Even in 1913 one judge used to ride his horse to the central courts in London.

Most middle and upper class houses had servants to do the housework.

POSH PEOPLE'S POLITE PARADISE

Before the First World War, life was much stricter in many ways than it is today, even for the upper classes. There were more unwritten rules about how you should and shouldn't behave:

You weren't meant to talk to people unless you'd been introduced to them first.

It was strictly against the rules for unmarried men and women to be alone together.

Women rode horses 'side saddle'. Their long skirts stopped them from dangling their legs on either side of the horse. It was almost unheard of for women to wear trousers, although a few wore 'bloomers' for cycling.

Posh (and not so posh) women had special 'at home' days when visitors called.

Almost everyone went to church on Sundays.

When a man visited, he carried his hat, gloves and stick into the drawing (living) room. It was thought rude to leave them in the hall.

NOT SO POSH - AND NOT QUITE PARADISE ...

Of course this world of servants and 'at home' days wasn't a paradise for everyone - not for the servants at any rate:

Most working people worked a full six day week and there were no paid holidays - except for servants, funnily enough.

Living conditions were often unhealthy and overcrowded.

Food was poor and, due to their bad diet, poor people tended to grow up much shorter than richer people. When the war came, the soldiers, who came from poorer families, were usually much shorter than their officers, who came from richer families.

A good education was very hard to come by unless you had money.

TOP DOG SNOBS

In 1914 each of the countries of Europe was ruled by a small group of 'top' people. The top people had money and power.

Germany was ruled by the Kaiser (Emperor) and his chief minister, the Chancellor. They were helped by the *junkers* (landed nobles), the generals and some big business men.

Britain was mainly ruled by a small group of top families through the Houses of Parliament. Britain was extremely rich and had a huge empire - it owned and controlled many other countries - so the top people were very rich indeed.

One of the problems with the world in 1914 was that nearly everyone thought their own country was better than anyone else's. Such ideas are dangerous - as World War I proved.

I'm a British lord. Britain is the richest country in the world and has the largest empire, so I'm better than anyone else.

I'm a German *junker* (noble). Britain is on the way out. Germany will soon be the most important country in the world, so I'm better than anyone else.

I'm a Russian lord. Russia is a huge, powerful country with a population almost equal to all the rest of Europe put together, so I'm better than anyone else.

I'm a French business man. France is the most civilized country in Europe and has a huge empire, so I'm better than anyone else.

I'm an American business man. I'm well away from any trouble and I'm getting richer by the minute, so I'm better than anyone else.

In fact, the pre-war world may have *seemed* like paradise to the soldiers who looked back on it from the horror of war, but this paradise wasn't ruled by angels at all. If any real angels were watching, they must have been worried ...

UNDER STARTER'S ORDERS

HOW IT BEGAN

THE BLACK HAND GANG

On 28 June 1914, Archduke Franz Ferdinand, the heir to the throne of the Austrian Empire  was visiting Bosnia, with his wife. Bosnia was a small country which had been swallowed up by the Austrian Empire only six years earlier.

> The majority of Bosnians were actually Serbs who wanted independence from Austria and to join up with next-door Serbia. Some Bosnian Serbs joined the Black Hand Gang, a secret society dedicated to winning freedom for Serbs everywhere.

Also in Bosnia was a young Serbian student called Gavrilo Princip, probably a member of the Black Hand Gang and certainly a member of 'Young Bosnia', another anti-Austrian movement. Gavrilo shot dead the Archduke and

---

The full name of the Austrian Empire was the *Austro-Hungarian* Empire because it included Hungary.

his wife in broad daylight in front of a horrified crowd in the centre of Sarajevo, the Bosnian capital - and started the First World War.

BASKET CASE

The Austrian Empire was a basket case - a basket of different countries and peoples - and most of them wanted to get out of the basket as soon as possible.

Back in Vienna, the capital of the Austrian Empire, old Emperor Franz Josef was soon swamped with letters from all the leaders of Europe. They said how sorry they were about the murder of the Archduke, his nephew. Josef wrote back and thanked them politely (even though he couldn't stand his nephew). There was more at stake than a family quarrel.

If Austria was seen to give way to mad Serbs like Gavrilo Princip and allowed Serbs to break away from the Empire, several other countries might try to break away as well. The Serbs must be punished as an example. That was why on 28 July 1914, Austria declared war on Serbia.

FRIENDS

Franz Josef felt that Austria was strong enough to go to war because Germany had promised to back him up. Germany was a big, powerful country. But even so, Austria were taking a huge risk ...

Would the Russians come to the aid of their friends the Serbs?

Would the French come to the aid of their friends the Russians?

Would the British come to the aid of the French?

Oh well, the Austrians went ahead anyway.

NOT VERY GOOD KNITTING

In 1914 all the big European countries were tied up in two great 'alliances'. (Groups of allies, see page 10.)

The 'allies' had promised to defend each other in case of attack on one of their members. This meant that if any two countries from different alliances started

BRITAIN: POPULATION 45 MILLION, POWERFUL NAVY BUT A SMALL ARMY OF ONLY 250,000 SOLDIERS.

GERMANY: POPULATION 70 MILLION, AN ARMY OF 850,000 SOLDIERS

FRANCE: POPULATION 35 MILLION, AN ARMY OF 700,000 SOLDIERS

ITALY: POPULATION 35 MILLION

■ Central Powers in 1914
▦ Joined the Central Powers soon after

fighting, all the rest were pretty well bound to be drawn in. Europe was tied up like a piece of knitting. Once it started to unravel, nothing could stop it.

RUSSIA: A VAST POPULATION, AND AN ARMY OF AROUND 1 MILLION SOLDIERS

AUSTRO-HUNGARIAN EMPIRE: POPULATION 50 MILLION, AN ARMY OF 450,000 SOLDIERS

SERBIA

BULGARIA

TURKEY: POPULATION PERHAPS 20 MILLION, AN ARMY OF 210,000 SOLDIERS

ROYAL RELATIONS

Most of Europe's monarchs were related to each other. This should have helped to sort problems out, but it didn't. The monarchs were either mad, stupid or proud - or all three.

Kaiser Wilhelm of Germany (1859-1941) was a grandson of Queen Victoria and a cousin of the British king, but he loathed the British. He had a withered left arm and a big moustache which was waxed by his special barber every morning. He was mad, proud - and nasty. He liked to hurt people with his extra-strong handshake (with his right hand naturally). He was also stupid and spoiled. The famous German Chancellor Bismarck said that 'Wilhelm would have liked to have had a birthday every day'. Wilhelm sacked Bismarck in 1890.

Czar Nicholas II of Russia (1868-1918) tried to run his enormous empire single handed because he believed that his power was given to him by God, but he was too stupid to make a good job of it. He liked keeping fit and loved to wear fancy military uniforms.

Victoria was Queen of Great Britain and Ireland 1837-1901.

Franz Josef I, Emperor of Austria-Hungary (1830-1916) wasn't mad, stupid or proud. He was just incredibly old. He died before the war was over.

George V of Great Britain (1865-1936) wasn't mad or stupid - but he was very proud of his country.

THE KNITTING UNRAVELS

After Austria declared war on Serbia, nothing much happened for a couple of days. At the time both President Poincaré of France and Kaiser Wilhelm were on ships sailing back to their own countries, and the Austrian Emperor Franz Josef was actually on holiday. But then, after they all got home, things happened very fast indeed.

- ⚝ *28 July*, Austria declared war on Serbia.
- ⚝ *1 August*, Germany declared war on Russia.
- ⚝ *3 August*, Germany declared war on France.
- ⚝ *4 August*, Germany invaded neutral Belgium en route to France.
- ⚝ *4 August*, Britain came to the aid of Belgium and declared war on Germany.

As British Foreign Secretary, Lord Grey, put it:

The lamps are going out all over Europe: we shall not see them lit again in our lifetime.

ORDER YOUR STARTERS

There are three possible answers to each of the following questions: either correct, possible or just plain daft. The correct one should come first and the daft one should come last - put them in the right order.

(Answers on page 243.)

1 What did the Austrian Empire do to Bosnia?

a Demolished it

b Swallowed it up

c Declared war on it

2 What was the Black Hand Gang?

a A secret Serbian society

b A gang of Serbian miners

c A secret German society

3 What did Kaiser Wilhelm want every day?

a A new moustache

b A birthday

c A letter from Queen Victoria

IT'LL BE OVER BY CHRISTMAS

WAR FEVER
A ROOMFUL OF RUMOURS

When Britain declared war on Germany on 4 August 1914, the whole country became madly excited. The air was full of rumours:

A German grocer living in England had been caught selling poisoned food to his customers.

A German barber in England was planning to cut his customers' throats.

A massive naval battle had been fought in the North Sea.

German spies were everywhere, taking notes and photographs.

A secret Russian troop train had crossed England with drawn blinds, bound for France.

Actually, there was no need for rumours. Reality was bad enough. Germans living in Britain rushed to leave. It wasn't sensible to be a foreigner. 'Aliens', as foreigners are often called, lost their jobs and their homes were attacked. It was very unfair. Many were sent to 'internment camps' - prisons in all but name.

Richard Noschke had lived in Britain for twenty-five years. As a German he was sent to an internment camp in London. This is what he said:

I had made many friends as I had spent the best part of my life over there (in Britain) ... nearly all, with very few exceptions, have turned against me ...

WAR FEVER

As soon as war was declared, thousands upon thousands of British men rushed to join the army, including many from Scotland, Wales and Ireland, which was then part of Britain. The whole country became a giant recruiting station. 30,000 men per day were joining the army by the end of the first month. There was a *two mile* queue to join the Liverpool Scottish regiment.

Sometimes large groups of men from one type of work or from the same town all joined up together in what became known as 'Pals' Battalions'. Pals' battalions had names such as the 'Grimsby Chums'. There weren't enough uniforms to go round so men wore their everyday clothes. Everyone mucked in: business men rubbed shoulders with dustmen, and servants mixed with posh gentlemen. The playgrounds and parks of Britain rang to the sound of men learning to be soldiers.

Men allowed themselves to be swept up in war fever for all kinds of reasons.

They wanted to see if they would be brave enough.

They wanted to travel abroad.

They liked the idea of fresh air and adventure - especially if they had worked in a factory or an office.

War fever wasn't just a British disease. It raged all over Europe. Poets had a field day writing about it all. Over

29

1.5 million poems were written in Germany and Austria that August - that's 50,000 poems a day! Here's a pretty silly patriotic 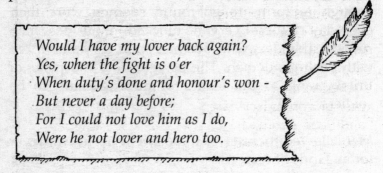 poem. It was printed on a postcard:

> Would I have my lover back again?
> Yes, when the fight is o'er
> When duty's done and honour's won -
> But never a day before;
> For I could not love him as I do,
> Were he not lover and hero too.

YOUR COUNTRY NEEDS YOU!

Going to war almost seemed like fun. After all, it would be 'over by Christmas'. Everyone said so. Well, not everyone - Lord Kitchener, the British Secretary of State for War, didn't think so. He thought that the war would be long and bloody. In the first months of the War, Kitchener led the British war effort almost single-handedly.

In 1914, Britain was the only large country which didn't have conscription . The British army was puny compared to other armies. So Kitchener prepared for the long struggle by raising brand new 'Kitchener armies' to help Britain's small regular army, which only had 250,000 men compared to Germany's 850,000, France's 700,000 and Russia's million. He did everything he could to encourage men to join up.

 Patriotism is love of one's country. A poem which is *patriotic* is about *patriotism*.

Conscription is compulsory military service.

54 million copies of his famous posters were printed - a picture of himself pointing with words such as: 'Britons. Join Your Country's Army! God Save the King'. Thanks to Kitchener, the British army put on muscle fast - a million men had joined up by the end of the year.

CAN WE JOIN?

Nowadays empires are out of fashion. That wasn't the case back in 1914. Both Britain and France had large empires and the British Empire at that time was the largest empire the world has ever known. British colonists  in Australia, New Zealand, Canada and South Africa joined up in their thousands. Likewise, soldiers from the Indian army and from other smaller countries were proud to fight for Britain or France.

As well as soldiers, the countries of Asia and Africa sent large armies of labourers to help the war effort. These men were not as well treated as the regular soldiers. African labourers in France only got half the pay of regular soldiers.

Many British people - English, Irish, Welsh and Scottish - had emigrated to countries in the British Empire, which is why most people in those countries speak English today. Such people were called *colonists* and their countries were called the *colonies*. In 1914 many of them still had close relatives in Britain and thought of themselves as British.

GRUNT, BOO, MOO

Animals were recruited as well. During the course of the war, 100,000 animals, mainly horses and camels, were sent from India to Mesopotamia in the Middle East, where 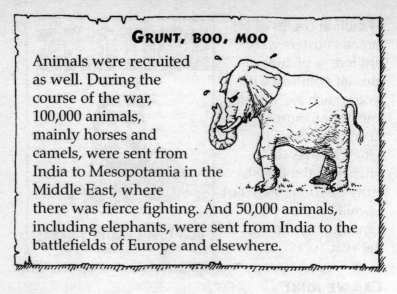 there was fierce fighting. And 50,000 animals, including elephants, were sent from India to the battlefields of Europe and elsewhere.

GOD SAYS

Not everyone was keen to join the army. Some men positively disagreed with the idea.

Posters asked girls to put pressure on their boyfriends to join with clever slogans:

Is your best boy wearing khaki? If not, don't you think he should be?

If he does not think you and your country are worth fighting for - do you think he is worthy of you?

The 'White Feather' movement was launched in Folkestone by an angry admiral. Young women were encouraged to dish out white feathers to young men in civilian 🦶 clothes as a badge of cowardice.

🦶 A civilian is anyone who is not in the armed forces.

Even the Church got in on the act. A Church of England chaplain thought that men who refused to fight ought to be drowned! It was the same all over. The Russian churches prayed:

Most gracious Lord, crush the enemy beneath our feet.

And a German pastor claimed that the slaying of the unworthy was an act of charity.

God must have been in a bit of a muddle about which side he was supposed to be on.

PASTY FACES

In Britain, men who thought it was wrong to fight became known as 'conscientious objectors', 'conchies' for short.

Conchies were savagely treated and many of them were forced to join the army anyway. Six thousand men were sent to British prisons and seventy died there through bad treatment.

However, far from being cowards, conchies were mostly very brave to stand up against public opinion at a time of war fever. In fact, many of them risked their lives driving ambulances in the battle zones anyway. They kept their spirits up through their own newspaper, called the *Dreadnought*. *Dreadnought*'s big scoop came later in the war: a letter from the famous poet, Siegfried Sassoon, who had won medals for bravery in France:

I believe the war is being deliberately prolonged by those who have the power to end it ...

Sassoon was sent to a mental hospital which was where a lot of conchies ended up. *Dreadnought* also reported cruelties, such as Field Punishment No.1 for British soldiers. Victims were strapped on to crucifixes on French main roads for up to two hours at a time.

Conchies disagreed with the war but how could the protests of a few thousand stop the catastrophe which was about to happen? All over Europe the new soldiers sang as they marched to the troop trains. In Germany they called their train the 'Paris Express' because they meant to conquer France. They were given garlands of flowers - like cattle before a sacrifice.

WAR FEVER

The date is August 1914. Britain has just declared war on Germany. Each correct answer wins you two degrees on the thermometer - can you reach fever pitch?
(Answers on page 243.)

1 What was the air full of in August 1914?

a German bombers
b Rumours
c The smell of gunpowder

2 What didn't Britain have when the war started?

a A powerful navy
b A border with Russia
c Conscription

3 What were conchies?

a A type of sea shell
b Men who objected to fighting because of their principles
c Men who volunteered to fight for their country

4 Where is this alien going?

a On holiday
b To an internment camp
c To join the British army

FEVER PITCH

100
99
98
97
96
95
94

IT'S A LONG, LONG WAY ...

LET BATTLE COMMENCE

ALL ABOARD!

British soldiers had to cross the English Channel before they could get to the 'front'  in France and Belgium, where the armies faced each other and the fighting would take place. Kaiser Wilhelm is said to have called the British army a 'contemptible little army' because it had so few soldiers in it compared to his own army. From then on, those first British soldiers to enter the war wore the name 'Old Contemptibles' with pride. One popular song of the time went:

> *Oh, we don't want to lose you*
> *But we think you ought to go ...*

It was about saying goodbye to soldiers going to war but the soldiers sang it too.

'*Front*' is short for 'front line' where the fighting took place. See pages 47-48.

Meanwhile, Kitchener's new recruits finished their training, first in Britain and then at Etaples, or 'Eat-Apples' as they called it, a tough training camp south of Boulogne in France. Eat-Apples was a grim place where bullying sergeant majors forced men to march up and down for hour after hour in the 'Bull-Ring', an enormous parade ground.

From Etaples, the journey to the front in France was long and hard, especially for soldiers who were new to soldiering. Simply moving so many men from A to B was a major problem. A division of twelve thousand men with all their gear took a *thousand* railway carriages.

Some French trains were just cattle trucks with straw on the floor. One old soldier described a truck with a notice on it: '40 men - 8 horses'. He spent the whole journey worrying that he was going to have to share his place with a horse!

Things weren't much better for the officers. One carriage had no door so the cold air blew in. The officers had to jump out every so often and run beside the train so aş to get warm.

When a division got to the end of the railway line, the soldiers had to get out and march the last bit of the journey to the battle grounds on foot - fifty minutes marching with ten minutes rest every hour. The packs on their backs weighed up to twenty-seven kilos. It was so tough that some men died on the march. Here's what Lance Corporal Mountfort of the Royal Fusiliers had to say about it:

The French roads are horrible. Through every village and for a mile or two on each side they are composed of great rough cobble stones. The nails of our boots step on them as on ice ... Our packs I cannot find words to describe. It is a cruel unnatural weight that no man should be called upon to carry.

The army gave the men tips on how to look after their feet:

Wash well with soap and water.

Dry well.

Rub inside of socks with soft or yellow soap.

Marching was awful and the soldiers tried to laugh away their troubles. One officer had to stop his men making 'excessively rude remarks to people who passed on bicycles'.

LET BATTLE COMMENCE

The Germans had a plan, called the *Schlieffen Plan* after the general who invented it. They planned to attack first - which was a bit like committing suicide in order to avoid dying, considering how many enemies they had. They would invade France through Belgium, beat the French and then attack the massive Russian army in the east.

German soldiers poured into Belgium.

The Germans took Brussels, the capital of Belgium, on 20 August 1914. King Albert of Belgium and his small army holed up in Antwerp near the coast opposite England to wait for the British.

The German occupation of Belgium was brutal. Thousands of Belgian civilians were shot in cold blood. Many Belgian men were herded into cattle trucks and sent to Germany. To cap it all, the Germans sacked the city of Louvain, deliberately burning its wonderful library of 230,000 books - and Belgium was neutral 👣!

When the citizens of Roubaix refused to make sandbags to protect the German trenches, the Germans shot some of them. The citizens said:

We shall not spin winding sheets 👣 *for our children.*

 A *neutral* country does not take part in any wars.

Winding sheets are used to wrap dead bodies.

British newspapers wrote stories about German 'frightfulness'. They said the Germans had built a corpse factory where Belgian bodies were melted down for fat. Most of what the newspapers wrote was bunkum, but British horror was real enough when the Germans executed an English nurse called Edith Cavill who had been helping Belgian soldiers to escape.

Back in Germany, the Germans also read about 'frightfulness' - except it wasn't German frightfulness, it was Belgian. One famous writer described Belgian priests who

... armed, lead bands of Belgian civilians committing every kind of atrocity ... eyes pierced and tongues cut off, of poisoned wells and other horrors.

That was all bunkum as well.

The first clash

On 23 August 1914, the German army came up against the British army for the first time, outside the little Belgian town of Mons. The small British Expeditionary Force fought bravely, but were forced to retreat. The Germans invaded France itself.

The Battle of the Marne was fought a little to the north of Paris starting on 6 September. It involved *two million* men. In that battle and in the next battle, known as the First Battle of Ypres, the French and the small British army stopped the Germans in their tracks.

ANGELS

Soldiers fighting for their lives sometimes became very superstitious. The story of the *Angels of Mons* was just that - a story - but it was believed as truth by many. British troops retreating from Mons were said to have been protected by the ghosts of medieval English bowmen from the Battle of Crecy, fought between the English and the French in 1346.

An Austrian volunteer in the German army at the First Battle of Ypres was given the Iron Cross and promoted to corporal for his bravery. He was a battalion 'runner', which meant that during the battle he was almost constantly in danger from allied fire. His name was Adolf Hitler - the same Hitler who led Germany during the Second World War.

After the Battle of the Marne, the Germans had a problem. After all, their plan had been to slice through Belgium, beat the French and British in the west, and then turn on the Russians in the east. Well, they hadn't beaten the French and the British, so what should they do next?

WHAT SHALL WE DO?

The Kaiser sweated over maps of the campaign in his headquarters in Berlin. He sacked his top general.

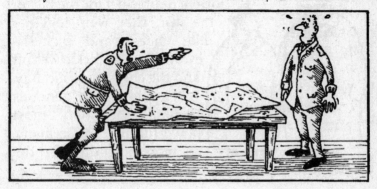

Then, on 30 August 1914, the Germans beat the Russians at the Battle of Tannenberg in East Germany. 30,000 Russians were killed, partly because they sent radio messages without putting them in code. Throughout the battle, the Germans knew exactly what the Russians were going to do before they did it.

ENTER THE DREADFUL DUO

However, the real victors of Tannenberg weren't the Germans. They were two German generals called Paul von Hindenburg and Erich Ludendorff. Paul von Hindenburg was commander of the German Eighth Army which won the battle of Tannenberg, and Ludendorff was his Chief of Staff. These two men joined up to form a double-act for the rest of the war. They went together like cheese and pickle - except that the pickle was off and the cheese was mouldy. Later, these two generals became the two most powerful men in Germany, more powerful than the Kaiser himself.

Hindenburg was a retired Prussian general. He came from an old noble family. He loved food, drink and cigars. He was very vain and liked to have his portrait painted as often as possible, usually in uniforms with lots of gold braid, decorations and buttons. 'A coat without a button is like a flower without a scent', he told one artist who painted him. What he was best at was never looking ruffled when the going got tough. He always appeared to be in command even when he didn't know what was going on - which happened quite a lot.

Erich Ludendorff was a cold fish - very cold. He had less sense of humour than a haddock. He wore a monocle (single eyeglass) and had a red face and droopy jowls which wobbled when he lost his temper. He was rude and cross most of the time, but he was also clever and very hard-working. Just the sort of man that Hindenburg needed. Their double-act worked like this:

Ludendorff did all the work.
Hindenburg looked important.

The funny thing is that Hindenburg *was* more important than Ludendorff - because he looked more

Prussia was a former German kingdom. Most of the original Prussian territories are now in Poland or Russia.

important. The Dreadful Duo rose to command all Germany's armies, and by the end of the war they ran Germany itself. It was only at the very end that they fell out - but more on that later.

LIFE IN MUD

TRENCH TROUBLES

MEANWHILE, IN THE MAZE ...

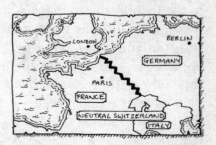

Christmas came and went. So did new year 1915. The line between the enemy armies stretched from the English Channel to the border of Switzerland. The soldiers dug trenches in which to hide from enemy fire, and the front line became a five-hundred-mile scar of trenches and defences dug across the heart of Europe.

The important thing was for the soldiers to keep their heads down and out of the way of bullets. Supplies had to be brought up, meals cooked, rifles cleaned - everything had to be done below ground level. Communicating trenches joined the firing trenches to support trenches further back, and joined them to the reserve lines which were still further back. British trenches followed a zigzag path to deaden the shock waves of exploding shells.

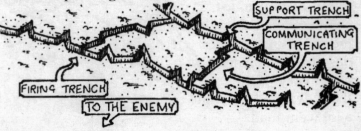

47

Because the trenches were below ground level, there was nowhere lower down for water to drain into if it rained. As a result, the trenches were often horribly muddy. Wooden 'duck boards' laid along the trench bottoms were supposed to help, but they too were often covered in mud. In the front firing trenches a step was carved into the earth on the side facing the enemy. Soldiers would step up on to this when they wanted to peer over or when it was their turn to fire at the enemy.

FIRESTEP

WOODEN DUCK BOARDS

Life in the trenches in the First World War was incredibly dangerous and uncomfortable. The conditions were truly horrible. Each month British soldiers spent one week in the firing line, one week in the support trenches, one week in the reserve lines and one week behind the lines. Any longer at the firing line and commanders feared that men might go mad or desert. As it turned out, very few of them deserted but quite a lot went mad.

ATTACKS AND SCRAPS

The whole point of being in France was to fight the enemy. The French and British wanted to drive the Germans back into Germany and the Germans wanted to conquer France. Either way, the target was to capture land from the opposition and thus force them to retreat.

In order to win land it was no good just staying in your trench - you had to *attack*. Throughout the war the generals kept organising major attacks when hundreds of thousands of men would be ordered to climb out of their trenches and attack the enemy's trenches - while the enemy naturally tried to stop them. If the attackers managed to hang on to a bit of land which had been controlled by the other side before the attack started, that was called a victory. Often the 'victories' involved pathetically narrow strips of land for which thousands of men paid with their lives.

It was impossible to organise major attacks all the time. They were hideously bloody and exhausting. To keep the men on their toes, and because there was a war going on, the generals organised raiding parties against enemy trenches, gunfire and sniping .
Sectors of the front where there was a lot of that sort of thing were called 'active'. Sectors where there wasn't were called 'cushy'. Most soldiers from both sides preferred the cushy sectors - understandably enough.

A *sniper* is an individual soldier with a rifle who aims at individual targets. What he does is called *sniping*.

LIFE - BUT NOT AS WE KNOW IT

If there were no major attacks going on, life in the trenches always settled down to a routine. Half an hour before sunrise might come the order to 'stand to' when each platoon stepped up to the firestep and sentries were posted. Then came breakfast. The day was filled with boring repair work, doing nothing and inspections and there was a second 'stand to' at dusk when the evening rations arrived.

ENTRANCE TO BUNKER

German commanders made sure their trenches were reasonably comfortable, but British commanders didn't believe in making trenches too comfortable in case the soldiers decided to settle down and didn't fight hard enough. This was a pretty nasty attitude to take towards men who, for most of the war anyway, had *volunteered* to fight for their country! Some trenches were so shallow that the men had to walk around stooped over, in order to avoid getting their heads shot off. If it rained, the trenches sloshed with mud. The soldiers shared the mud with trench rats, and with the bones of some of the millions of men who died in battle.

The bones were one of the most horrible things about the trenches. The bodies of soldiers who had died in earlier battles were often churned up again by artillery shells, so that some dead bodies were buried and reburied many times, during the course of the war.

It was hard to stay healthy. Soldiers' uniforms became infested with lice. They would try to kill them by running lighted matches down the seams, but nothing really worked.

Trench fever was a new and dangerous disease. Even worse was trench foot. This appalling illness was caused by spending weeks in cold, wet mud. Feet swelled up to two or three times normal size and went so numb that they could be run through by a bayonet without pain.

OFFICER MATERIAL

Young officers were expected to lead their men into battle. On average, a young officer arriving at the front could expect to live no more than two weeks. In the early days they went into battle with their white gloves on. The Germans could see who they were and so shot them first. These young officers were some of the real heroes. There were mutinies (revolts against authority) in all the other armies, but there were no real mutinies in the British army. The young officers shared the hardships of the common soldiers and many of them truly cared for the men under their command. Letters home from officers were full of requests for chocolate and other luxuries, not for themselves but for their men.

Officers and men were united in hating the generals and staff-officers back at headquarters. One young officer arranged for a trench dam to be 'accidentally' broken so that a general and his staff got covered in slime.

WEAPONS PARADE

A whole package of weapons was available to help the soldiers kill each other.

Artillery was positioned behind the lines. It fired over the heads of the soldiers in the firing line and into the enemy beyond. The biggest guns, such as 'Big Bertha' a type of German

gun which bombarded Paris late in the war, could fire up to 122 kilometres (76 miles) or further. The noise from these massive guns was so loud that artillery men might suffer concussion or bleeding ears.

Bayonets were pretty useless in an age of mechanised warfare, but most soldiers carried them.

The main rifle of the British army was the Lee Enfield.

Lewis guns were light machine guns, fired from the shoulder.

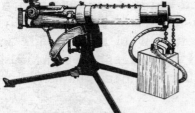

Vickers guns were heavy machine guns, fired from a tripod.

Mills bombs were hand grenades with handles. In July 1916 the British Expeditionary Force got through 800,000 Mills bombs per week.

The 'flying pig' was a 68 kg mortar. It could blast through almost any dugout.

Medium-sized mortars were called 'toffee apples' or 'Christmas puddings'.

GAS!

Gas was a new weapon in the Great War. It was first used by the Germans in April 1915 when they gassed a number of French Morrocan soldiers. The murky, greenish-yellow colour of chlorine stained the ground for days afterwards. Chlorine gas was followed by phosgene and then by mustard gas which were even more deadly. Gas caused blindness, suffocation and death. The Allies complained about it, but they copied the Germans all the same. By 1918, a quarter of all shells fired by the armies in France were gas shells.

In the early days, soldiers protected themselves as best they could. Socks soaked in urine and held over the face were quite effective against chlorine. Later they used nose clips and cotton wool mouth pads and finally they were issued with large, heavy gas masks which made them look like mutant elephants.

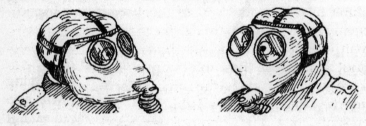

SINGING MACHINE GUNS

In the Middle Ages, '*nonesmannesland*' meant an area of land where ownership was unclear, then it came to mean a spot outside the walls of the city of London where executions took place. In the Great War, 'no man's land' came to mean the strip of dead ground between the opposing trenches, a ghastly dead place where wounded men often bled to death because it was too dangerous to rescue them. This dead strip of land could be several hundred metres wide, but more often it was less than that. Sometimes the trenches of the opposing armies might only be separated by ten or twenty metres, and sometimes they even ran through the ruins of the same house. When that happened, the men could hear the smallest rustle of their enemies' clothing.

If two armies face each other for over five hundred miles at such close range, there's one thing you can't stop, and it's not killing - it's laughter. The soldiers were human beings after all, and although they had been taught to hate each other before they arrived, it didn't take long for most of them to realise that the enemy were men very much like themselves. On more than one occasion, the war broke down completely. Most famous of these occasions was the Christmas truce of 1914 when the men spilled out of their trenches into no man's land. They gave each other presents, there was a football game and a joint burial service. This is how Rifleman Dick Harvey described it:

The Germans ... they used to walk about on top with our chaps, exchanging cigarettes, tobacco and shaking hands with us. It was a curious sight to see them strolling about in No Man's Land as though war was the last thing they thought about ...

The generals were very cross and it never happened quite like that again.

Quite a few Germans spoke English having worked as waiters in London before the war. They would shout across for news of English football results, or ask the British soldiers to take messages to the Germans' girlfriends in London. One German soldier called across:

It is I Fritz, the bunmaker of London. What is the football news? ... Are you soon going home on leave? Then call at 224 Tottenham Court Road and give my love to Miss Sarah Jones.

There were concerts when the men from each side would sing to each other. Good musicians were popular - no matter which army they belonged to.

A favourite game was for machine gunners to let off bursts of bullets to the rhythm of popular songs. Everyone had to guess what songs they were. A dozen

or more machine guns might join
in the chorus. The British gave
names to Germans who were
good at it:

> *Duckboard Dick*
>
> *Parapet Joe*
>
> *Happy Harry*

LIVE AND LET DIE

Douglas Haig (commander of British armies in
France, see page 62) believed in an 'active
front' policy and thought that the men
should keep fighting all the time. So the
front had dangerous sectors where the
fighting never stopped. 'Fire eaters' were
men who wanted to fight. They
weren't popular because the enemy
might fight back! The Scottish
regiments tended to be full of fire
eaters. The Germans called them 'women
from hell' because of their kilts .

Some soldiers actually *enjoyed* fighting. This is what
Lieutenant Colyer had to say about it:

*How different it feels to be doing something! Back there in the
trenches I feel like a rat in a trap ... I don't feel any more
frightened of Fritz (the Germans) than if I were playing hide
and seek in the dark with him ...*

Kilts weren't a good uniform for the trenches. It was found that soldiers
in kilts were more likely to get frostbite and other illnesses. Most Scottish
regiments gave up wearing them.

LIVE AND LET LIVE

On 'cushy' sectors there was almost no fighting at all. Generals didn't approve of cushy sectors but they couldn't do much about them. In cushy sectors, the men on both sides believed in 'live and let live' - they agreed not to kill each other. Above all, they agreed not to fire at each other's toilets and never to fire during breakfast. There were lots of ways of agreeing:

Always fire your guns at the same place at the same time every day. The enemy will soon realise what you're up to and keep out of the way.

Make lots of noise during a raid so the enemy can get out of the way.

Always aim high if an officer orders you to fire your rifle.

Throw over a friendly message tied to a stone, such as this one from some Germans:

We are going to send an 18 kg bomb. We have got to do this but we don't want to - we will whistle first to warn you.

After one burst of artillery fire, a brave German stood up outside his trench and shouted:

We're very sorry about that. We hope no one was hurt. It's not our fault, it's that damn Prussian artillery.

An officer once asked a British soldier why he didn't shoot at an elderly German soldier with a bald head and long white beard whose head was sticking up above the German trenches and made an easy target. The British soldier replied:

Why lord bless you sir, he's never done me any harm!

SOAP AND FOOTBALL

Soldiers were able to relax behind the lines. There the sick and the wounded were treated in field hospitals and the well could enjoy the British soldiers' favourite pastimes of theatre (home-made) and football. There were hundreds of football teams and leagues up and down the front.

Behind the trenches the soldiers found another world, a world where life was almost normal. A world where the French went about their everyday business. In fact British soldiers were amazed at how French farmers would tend their fields almost within shell shot of the Germans. In little French villages the British soldiers could find *estaminets*, small bars where they drank wine - the water was mostly undrinkable. In fact about all that French civilians used water for was washing. Given half a chance the British were no different. Special bath houses were set up for the troops where they could shower in scalding hot water and put on clean clothes without lice - if they were lucky.

CATASTROPHE

As bad as it gets

Bullets v. flesh

The big battles of the First World War were among the most terrible things that human beings have ever deliberately done to each other. The reason lies partly in the weapons of the soldiers but mostly in the stupidity of the commanders.

One machine gun could kill a line of soldiers in seconds. They had no armour to protect them from the bullets, as armour had once protected soldiers from swords or arrows. So *attack* was difficult because the attackers couldn't defend themselves against the machine guns of the *defenders* (the defenders had their trenches). General Kitchener understood what this meant - that against machine guns, attack was little better than suicide - but he didn't know what to do about it.

Yet there seemed to be no way to win the war other than by attacking the enemy trenches on foot ('going over the top'). Each time the generals gave the order to attack, they knew that thousands of men would die.

It was hopeless. Back home, the politicians complained about the stalemate or the deaths, and sometimes about both. Then on 17 December 1915, they appointed a new man to take over command of the British armies in France. Kitchener at least understood the problem - General Douglas Haig couldn't really see the problem at all.

Like Kitchener, Douglas Haig realised that the war would go on a great deal longer than most people hoped. Unlike Kitchener, he thought it was possible to win it - so long as the British and their French allies had enough guns and ammunition to do the job. In other words, he was ready to command a ghastly slogging match which would cost millions of lives.

THE GRINDING MACHINE

In December 1915, after the slogging match had gone on for over twelve months, the German commanders decided that they would have to 'bleed France white' - the French army was still far larger than the British. It was just a question of numbers: Germany had more men than France, so the French would have to give up first. If necessary, the war would be over when the last German killed the last Frenchman.

This horrible idea was known as 'attrition' and for a

while generals on both sides of the war believed in it. The Germans attacked the fortress of Verdun 200 km (125 m) to the east of Paris, which they knew the French would defend at all costs. The plan was that Verdun would be a killing ground where German forces would slowly destroy the French.

The battle started in February 1916. A *million* German shells  fell on the first day alone. Another million were fired before the German troops attacked. However, to their amazement they found that some French troops had survived the shells and were waiting for them.

And so it went on. For ten dreadful months the Germans flung themselves against the French defences and the French fought back like cornered rats. The French lost *half a million* men - dead, wounded or missing; German losses weren't much better. Verdun became known as the 'mill' or the 'grinding machine'. No one could stay in that hell for long without cracking, so the French commanders sent in new troops and shipped out survivors for a rest - like a giant conveyor belt. By the end of the Battle of Verdun, almost the entire French army had fought in it.

 Shells are large explosive missiles fired from guns.

ORDERS IS ORDERS

First World War armies were too big for their boots - literally. Headquarters, where the generals made their plans and gave their orders, were usually far behind the front line, out of reach of enemy artillery fire. It took ages for an order from headquarters to reach soldiers at the front. No way could a commander decide on an attack and expect it to be carried out the same day. To make matters worse, telephone lines near the front were often cut by shell fire, so to send orders to their troops, generals often had to use runners - in boots - or pigeons.

The size of the armies meant that orders became incredibly complicated. Each group of soldiers, each battery of guns, each group of supply waggons had to be told exactly where to go and what to do. A major attack using tanks, planes, guns and troops needed hundreds, if not thousands, of orders to set in motion. Before the Battle of the Somme, one British headquarters produced a *seventy-six page* plan of attack, backed up by a 365 page supplement!

A HOST OF BEES

Verdun was a French nightmare. The Battle of the Somme was a British nightmare - and a German one. In July 1916, Haig ordered a massive attack across the river Somme in western France so as to draw the Germans away from Verdun and give the French a chance to recover.

The roar of the British guns was so loud that it could be heard back in England. Even the rats in the German trenches panicked.

Well, the rats panicked but not the Germans themselves. They hid in their bunkers, nine metres

Bunkers were underground rooms which the soldiers carved out of the ground. They gave protection from shell fire and rain.

underground, and waited for the bombardment to finish. On 1 June, a beautiful sunny day, the guns fell silent and at the word of command, the British soldiers began the attack. They climbed out of their trenches - going 'over the top' was what they called it - and walked into a blizzard of German machine gun bullets.

One soldier described the sound of the bullets as like the humming of 'hosts of bees'. Photographs show the British soldiers walking forward into the bullets bent forwards almost as if they are walking into a snow storm. *60,000* British soldiers were killed on the first day alone - that's probably around *eighty lives per minute* during the fighting.

The Battle of the Somme raged for over five months - and at the end of it all, the line between the armies was roughly where it had been at the beginning. By the time it was over in November 1916, the Germans had lost 750,000 men, the British 420,000 and the French 195,000.

It was the grim duty of officers to write to the families of the dead. After the Battle of the Somme, people came to dread any knock at the door in case it brought bad news:

Dear Sir,
It is my painful duty to acquaint you of the death of your son killed in action on ... there is little comfort that I can add ...

And the women wore black

Verdun and the Somme changed how people saw the war. The newspapers could no longer pretend that it was all a wonderful adventure. In Britain, crowds gathered round the offices of their local newspapers and demanded to be told the truth. Lists of the dead began to fill the pages, often with photographs of the young men who had died. Whole streets drew their curtains in mourning. The country looked dingy. Most people wore dark clothes because they were in mourning, and it became unpatriotic to look smart. Smartly-dressed people were jostled in the street.

The Somme also signalled the end of the pals' battalions. The towns where they'd been recruited were devastated by the battle. Some towns lost nearly all their young men in a few short hours of fighting. It was thought better to spread the losses around in future.

DREADFUL DUO (CONTINUED)

Hindenburg and Ludendorff, the victors of Tannenberg, wanted to command all the German armies. After Verdun, Hindenburg became chief of the 'Great General Staff' and Ludendorff became 'First Quartermaster General'. It was even agreed that Hindenburg could give orders in the Kaiser's name without asking him first. The reign of the Duo had begun.

The Kaiser didn't like the Dreadful Duo, but they were popular and he wasn't. While German soldiers were dying by the thousand at Verdun he moved into a different palace, (he had seventy-six of them including castles and hunting lodges) and his life went on as before - like one long holiday. It was all you could expect from a mad man. His favourite hobby was sawing wood. He took up hunting and held champagne dinners for victory. As one German general put it: 'he performed none of the duties of a monarch'.

FRANCE 1917

Ludendorff wisely ordered his troops to dig in and let the enemy attack them, rather than do the attacking themselves. Early in 1917 the German army in France retreated behind the 'Hindenburg line', a new network of trenches.

The retreating Germans laid waste to the land as they left it. Villages and towns were sacked, roads were mined, buildings booby-trapped, wells ruined with horse manure, and most of the people who lived in the area were shipped off to Germany or Belgium.

The French general Nivelle ordered a new attack. The Battle of Chemin des Dames, called after a road to the north of Rheims, was yet another blood bath. The Germans fought back from their new trenches and the French attackers were mown down like grass before a lawn mower. The French won just 500 metres of land and lost 270,000 men in the process.

The horror of seeing large numbers of dead bodies shocked even hardened soldiers. Take this description by a Captain Leetham in 1916:

... the dead were stretched out on one side, one on top of the other, six feet high. I thought at the time I should never get the peculiar, disgusting smell of warm human blood heated by the sun out of my nostrils.

PASSCHENDAELE - THE VICTORY OF MUD

British General Haig could
have learned from the French
disaster at Chemin des
Dames. But no - he ordered an
all-out British attack.

First, British soldiers dug nineteen tunnels beneath the
German lines along Messine ridge, south of Ypres, in
Belgium. They packed them with over *half a million kilos* of
high explosive.

On 7 June 1917, a massive explosion ripped through the
German trenches, killing or wounding twenty thousand
men in seconds. It was heard 209 kilometres (130 miles)
away in London. Then the British guns opened up and,
while the ground was still trembling, 80,000 British
soldiers charged out of their trenches. It was a British
victory; it was also the start of a journey into hell.

The actual Third Battle of Ypres, otherwise known as *Passchendaele*, began on 31 July 1917 in the same area. For two weeks before it started, the British guns rained 4.5 million shells on the Germans. This turned out to be a pretty good warning to the Germans that an attack was coming. So when the British attacked, they too were mown down in their thousands.

Haig had been warned to expect heavy rain in that area in August, but he chose to ignore the warning. The guns and the rain churned the battlefield into a huge sea of mud. It was so deep that men and horses drowned in it.

When the attack fizzled out four months later, just outside the village of Passchendaele, the British had gained just over 7 kilometres (4 miles) of ground - and paid for it with the lives of 324,000 men.

IN THE AIR

BIPLANES AND AIRSHIPS

ZEPPELINS

Planes had never been used in war before the First World War. In fact, the first manned flight had only taken place in 1903, so they were a very recent invention. At the start of the war, the French had just 136 and the Germans 180. The British had even less. They proved to be so useful that, by the end, France alone was building more than 136 planes *per day*.

To begin with, the Germans preferred airships. These gas-filled, lighter-than-air monsters weren't as fast as aeroplanes, but they could carry far more bombs and fly much higher. The best were designed by Count von Zeppelin. When they appeared over the British skies people would shout: 'Zeps! Zeps!' as they ran for cover.

198 METRES

2 MILLION CUBIC FEET OF HYDROGEN

ENGINE SOUNDED LIKE A TRAM WITH RUSTY WHEELS

MAXIMUM SPEED 40 KPH (30 MPH)

At the start of the air war, even the poor mad Kaiser had doubts about dropping bombs on civilians miles behind the scene of battle. But early in 1915, he overcame his doubts and allowed zeppelins to carry out their first bombing mission. They were told to bomb only military targets and to be especially careful not to hit any royal palaces.

The first two raiders were spotted high above East Anglia in January 1915, so high up that they looked like 'two bright stars'. The crash of the bombs from the stillness of the sky was shocking. Four people died. Despite the frightfulness and the danger, there was something marvellous about zeppelins. They were so big and they floated so lazily above the rooftops, as if they had all the time in the world. People came out of their houses to watch.

The first zeppelins could only fly as far as East Anglia, but improved designs soon reached London. Curiosity then gave way to panic, but only for a while. A new explosive bullet was invented and on 2 September 1916, one of these bullets hit its target for the first time. A huge fireball from the burning gas lit the sky above London. It was so bright that you could read a newspaper by its light twenty miles away. The stricken airship turned nose down and the pilot jumped from his gondola to escape the flames. To no avail: his spread-eagled body formed a crater in the soil several centimetres deep. That day spelled the end of airships.

LIGHTS OUT!

Meanwhile the Germans had developed a new deadly weapon - the long distance bomber. The first bomber attack on London came in 1916. Next year, twin-engined Gothas raided deep over England like swarms of 'bright silver insects'.

The bombers caused mayhem and the British had to develop new defences.

Listening posts (which looked like giant ear trumpets) were set up along the coast to give advance warning.

Boy scouts and girl guides worked as messengers, stretcher bearers and signallers during air raids.

Each night there was a total blackout across Britain. All windows were covered and no street lights were lit. German pilots heading for London prayed for moonlight so that they could follow the course of the silvery River Thames to their target.

WINGS OF FIRE

Where aeroplanes were most useful was over the battlefields of France. They brought back priceless information about enemy positions. Control of the skies had become vitally important for the armies underneath. During the course of the war, 50,000 young men met their deaths in the air. Incredibly brave pilots often shot at each other from less than a hundred metres apart. By 1917, a new pilot arriving in the war zone was not expected to survive more than *seventeen* days. This wasn't helped by the fact that parachutes weren't allowed until the very end of the war, in case airmen were tempted to bail out too soon. The stupidity of World War I commanders was almost boundless.

GENTLEMEN OF THE AIR

Although aircraft were new, the war in the air was in some ways more old fashioned and good-mannered than war on the ground.

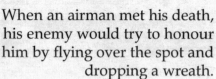

Pilots would stop firing at an enemy plane once it was obviously out of action.

When an airman met his death, his enemy would try to honour him by flying over the spot and dropping a wreath.

Flying very high to avoid anti-aircraft fire, pilots would drop messages in metal canisters behind enemy lines asking for news of missing men. Such messages nearly always got a reply.

If an airman had to land in enemy territory, he was normally well treated. In case of capture, most airmen flew with a parcel of such things as pyjamas, toothpaste, cigarettes and money.

PLANES OF FAME

Sopwith camel - British

Fokker triplane - German. Fokkers were the first planes to make sure that machine gun fire was in time with the propellor blades so that the bullets didn't hit the blades. Before that, machine guns had to be fired from the side at an angle.

Nieuport - French

Spad - British

Albatross - German

Sopwith pup - British

THE NARROW ESCAPE OF MCLEOD AND HAMMOND.

In 1918, both Alan McLeod and his 'observer', Arthur Hammond were attacked by seven German triplanes.

They shot down two enemy planes, but both airmen were wounded.

Their petrol tank was set alight, setting fire to McLeod's wicker seat.

McLeod throttled back and pushed the joystick forward. He stepped out on to the lower wing to avoid the fire - and kept on flying.

One German aircraft attacked again. The floor below Hammond's cockpit gave way as he struggled to fire back.

Wounded again, Hammond straddled the fuselage and drove off their attacker with his machine gun.

McLeod flew in a curve so that the flames and smoke were blown away from them both.

They landed in a bomb crater. Both survived, although Hammond was wounded in five places.

ACES

The best pilots were called 'aces'. Most famous of all the aces was the German pilot, Baron von Richthofen, otherwise known as the 'Red Baron' because his aircraft was painted red. Von Richthofen's 'circus' of up to thirty aircraft was deadly. He himself shot down eighty enemy aircraft before he was killed by a British airman on 21 April 1918. By then he had become as famous as a sports star. His body was laid out in a British hangar and hundreds of British soldiers and sailors filed past it to pay their respects.

Pilots were mostly very young and, being youngsters, they sometimes got up to mad adventures. New Zealander Keith Park and his observer Puggy Shone bombed the beach at Ostend with oranges where German officers were sitting with their girlfriends.

Later they bombed a German aerodrome with a football painted bright red with streamers tied to it. Their 'bouncing' bomb caused havoc but no injuries.

AIR SLIPS

There's been a bit of a slip-up in each of these pictures. What's wrong with them?
(Answers on page 243.)

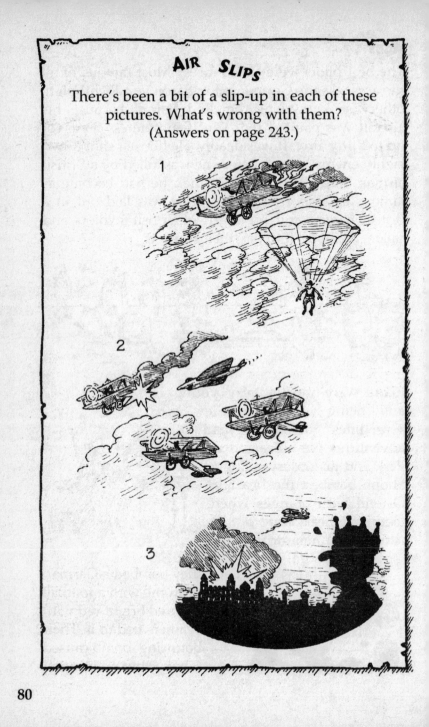

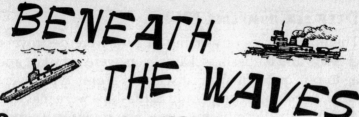

BENEATH THE WAVES

BILGE RATS AND KIPPERS

BILGE RATS

Airmen were aces, soldiers were 'leather-necks' (at least as far as sailors were concerned) and sailors were 'bilge-rats ⟋'. There were a lot of bilge rats in the British Royal Navy in 1914. It was then the largest navy in the world. And there were even more bilge rats in the British Merchant Navy, which was also the largest in the world - more than twice as large as the merchant navies of all the other countries which fought in the Great War put together.

Even before the war, the Germans hadn't liked the fact that the British were so strong at sea. As we've seen, the German leadership believed that Germany too had a right to an empire, to a 'place in the Sun' as they put it. They could never hope to win such an empire without a strong navy of their own. Under the leadership of stern, fork-bearded Admiral Tirpitz, they set out to build one. Britain had no intention of letting them catch up, and the arms race which followed had helped to heat the war fever of 1914.

Bilge water is filthy water that collects in the bilge, the bottom of a ship.

DEEP SEA DUMPLING 1914

The main classes of warship in 1914 were destroyers, cruisers and battleships. Destroyers were very fast and agile but quite small. Cruisers of various types were large, fast fighting ships, and battleships were massive. And of all battleships, the Dreadnought class of super-battleship was most feared. Dreadnoughts were named after *HMS Dreadnought*, launched in 1906. She had twelve massive guns which could fire over 16 kilometres (10 miles) and she displaced 22,000 tons of water. Nothing could stand up to a Dreadnought.

BRITISH NAVY: 65 BATTLESHIPS, 120 CRUISERS, PLUS MANY SMALLER SHIPS SUCH AS DESTROYERS

GERMAN NAVY: 40 BATTLESHIPS, 57 CRUISERS, PLUS SMALLER SHIPS

FRENCH NAVY: 28 BATTLESHIPS, 34 CRUISERS PLUS SMALLER SHIPS

The German commanders were well aware that the British navy was more powerful than their own, so the German navy spent almost the entire war holed up in its base at Wilhelmshaven. As a result, there was only one major battle between the main British and German fleets, and that didn't happen until the end of May 1916. There's never been a sea battle of a similar size since. It involved 250 warships.

THE BATTLE OF JUTLAND

On 31 May 1916, British scouting ships off Jutland Bank in the North Sea made contact with German ships. They had no idea that the German fleet was in the area.

The battle started with a fight between cruisers which the Germans got the better of. After that the main fleets clashed.

The main battle lasted only a few minutes but it was spectacular. The guns of the massed battleships and cruisers sent waterspouts gushing up to sixty metres into the air. Direct hits produced vast columns of smoke and debris. The German Admiral soon realised that he was out-gunned. The Germans turned away under a smoke screen and scuttled back to base as fast as they could. From that time on, the German fleet never challenged the British fleet again, not in the First World War anyway. The British had won the argument even if they hadn't triumphed in the battle itself.

The British First Sea Lord in 1915 was Admiral John Fisher. Fisher hated sport, perhaps due to the fact that when young he had shot a butler in mistake for a rabbit.

KILLER KIPPERS

The mighty Dreadnoughts were a threat which were never fully used. Not so 'kippers', or 'tinfish', as submarines were known in the Royal Navy. And especially not German kippers.

German submarines were better designed than British submarines. Even at the start of the war, the best German vessels could diesel at full speed for up to 6,500 kilometres (4000 miles), submerge in less than two minutes to a depth of 30-60 metres, and travel for up to 130 kilometres (80 miles) underwater. In other words, they could pop up almost anywhere, let off their torpedoes and scarper before the British had time to react.

On 22 September 1914, a German submarine, U-9 👣, was cruising off the coast of Holland when her captain spied three British cruisers, *HMS Aboukir*, *Cressy* and

👣 *U-boats* were German submarines. The 'U' is short for *Unterseeboot*, meaning 'under-sea ship'.

Hogue. They were very powerful ships and one measly submarine should have been no match for them.

U-9 sank the lot in one hour before breakfast. 1,459 men died, more men than all the British sailors who had died during the entire Battle of Trafalgar over a hundred years before.

Less than a month later, a single German U-boat was spotted in a Scottish loch. After their experience off Holland, the British took no chances. Due to this one U-boat, Scapa Flow, the deep-water base of the British fleet, was declared unsafe and the entire fleet was moved to Northern Ireland until Scapa Flow could be made secure. From then on, apart from the Battle of

Jutland, the mighty British navy spent almost all of the War holed up in Scapa Flow, like some monstrous guard dog that couldn't be allowed out of its kennel.

Most submarines used diesel on the surface, although to start with the French preferred steam. But both diesel and steam engines are useless under water because they need air to burn fuel. During the First and Second World Wars, submarines ran on electric motors powered by huge batteries when submerged.

Biggest of all submarines were the British K-boats. K-boats were massive - and pretty useless. Only seventeen K-boats were built - they had sixteen bad accidents and eight disasters. K-boats were far too long and narrow. The Germans had a joke about them:

MY END IS DIVING - WHAT THE HELL IS YOUR END DOING?

LIFE IN A KIPPER

Early submarines were hideously uncomfortable.

Their long, thin hulls rolled badly. Water from the conning tower (the bit that sticks up in the middle of a submarine) mixed with food and vomit from sick submariners and sloshed from side to side.

The underwater toilets stank so horribly that some crew members used to take medicines to stop themselves using them.

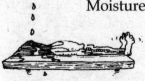

Moisture condensed on the steel walls. It would drop onto the faces of sleeping men. It was common practice to sleep with a rubber sheet over the face.

Lack of bunks on British submarines meant that taking turns with bunks was often unavoidable.

Men could get 'drunk' on gasoline fumes from the engines. Mice were kept on board. Their squeaking let the sailors know if any gasoline escaped.

Pressure could build up under water. It was sensible to hold on to the captain's legs when he opened the hatch, to stop him shooting out like a cork from a bottle.

A SINK IN THE DRINK

By 1917 the U-boats were sinking an average of *630,000 tons* of allied shipping per month. On the other hand, the British navy was strong enough to blockade Germany so that almost no goods or food got through by sea. Both countries were being strangled. The question was: who would strangle who first? For quite a while it looked as though Britain might be the loser. The British fought back as best they could:

In clear water a submarine could be seen at quite a depth. British submarines towed 'blimps' or observation balloons, which floated high up. The observer in the small cage could spot U-boats from a distance.

At the beginning of the war, some British torpedo boats carried lengths of copper wire with a noose on the end. The idea was to lasso the enemy's periscope.

Q-boats were designed to look like harmless merchant or fishing vessels. However, if a U-boat attacked one of them the Q-boat quickly showed her teeth.

Gunfire and ramming were thought to be the best ways to sink a U-boat.

👣 A *periscope* is a device which allows you to see round corners (or above the surface if you're under water), using mirrors to reflect light. They were also used to see over the top of trenches without exposing the head of the looker to enemy fire.

Convoy ahoy!

At last, on 30 April 1917, Britain came up with an answer to submarines - convoys. A convoy consisted of a large number of merchant ships protected by warships. They all sailed together. Lloyd George, the British Prime Minister had been suggesting this for years, as had others such as Winston Churchill, but the admirals had claimed that convoys would be sitting targets for the U-boats. It really was extraordinary how foolish First World War commanders could be.

Almost at once Allied losses at sea started to fall. Convoys had two big advantages:

1. Allied merchant ships were no longer scattered all over the oceans. It was no longer possible for a U-boat to cruise about and expect to bump into its prey by chance. Now the U-boats often failed to bump into anything at all.
2. When a U-boat attacked a convoy, it often only got in one shot, then it had to dive fast or the naval destroyers would sink it.

All in all, convoys were a big success. Between May and November 1918, 1,142 ships carrying 2,079,880

American soldiers plus food and other supplies crossed the Atlantic in convoy, and only one was lost.

THE LOSING OF THE LUSITANIA

On 7 May 1915, the British liner, *Lusitania*, was steaming home to Liverpool from New York. She had two thousand passengers on board and a cargo of ammunition for the British war effort, although that was a secret at the time. The *Lusitania* had just rounded the southern tip of Ireland when she was spotted by the submarine U-20, captained by blond, handsome Walter Schweiger.

Schweiger was no monster but he had his orders. At that time, German submarines were under orders to attack all shipping in the seas around the British Isles and they didn't have to give any warning. Schweiger's first torpedo set off a massive explosion on board the great liner, which keeled over and sank within eighteen minutes. 1,198 people died that day, including 94 children and 128 Americans.

It was the Americans who really mattered. At that time America was neutral, but with the loss of the Lusitania American public opinion started to shift in favour of the Allies. To make matters worse, the German government struck a special medal to gloat over the sinking. The medal was copied in large numbers in America and Britain as proof of yet more German 'frightfulness'.

Blindly, the Germans torpedoed another passenger liner, the *Arabic*, that August, killing three more Americans. There were howls of outrage. For a while the Germans were forced to be more careful, and at least not to attack without warning.

However, by 1917 the Germans were desperately short of food due to the British blockade. Their only chance still seemed to be to starve Britain into asking for peace. On 1 February they declared unrestricted submarine warfare. This was a dangerous move because it was bound to anger the Americans even more.

On 3 February America cut all relations with Germany, and by April, Germany and America were at war.

HOME AT LAST

BACK IN BRITAIN

THE GREEN DREAM

Soldiers in the trenches in France longed for home leave , to be back in 'Blighty' as they called Britain. Unfortunately, the reality of home leave never quite lived up to the dream. After the hell of the trenches, the lush, green English countryside could seem overwhelmingly beautiful at first, but soldiers found it difficult to fit back into ordinary life. The people back home sounded so *warlike*. Hating was easy from far away. It was much harder to hate the enemy if you had sung to him at night and you knew that he suffered as you did. As one soldier put it: 'the further you get from the battle line, the more offensive are the people you meet'.

In the armed forces 'leave' means permission to be absent from duty.

And did those civilians hate! The Germans even had a 'song of hate'. It went like this:

We will never forgo our hate
We have all but a single hate
We love one, we hate one.
We have one foe and one alone - England!

Meanwhile the bishop of London preached a sermon of hate:

We are banded in a
great crusade - we
cannot deny it - to kill
Germans ... to kill the
good as well as the bad,
to kill the young men
as well as the old ...

DO YOUR BIT

There was no escape from war. Even if you were home on leave, it was all around you. Everyone 'did their bit' for the war effort.

In Germany, school children were told to collect nettles to make into nettle fibre for weaving cloth.

In Britain, schools ran jumble sales and concerts. People collected silver paper and rags to melt down for metal and to make cloth.

There were 'tank banks' to help raise money for arms. A 'Feed the Guns' campaign in London raised £1 million. It was opened by six girls who had lost their boyfriends. They stood by a tank which had the mud of France still on it.

Railway lines were pulled up to be melted down for guns and ammunition.

FOOD - IF YOU CAN GET IT!

Both Germany and Britain ran short of food. It was worst for Germany, where three quarters of a million people died of starvation during the war, especially during the terrible 'turnip winter' of 1917. They imposed a tax on cats in Dresden since cats eat food. Life was hard in Britain too. Every scrap of land that could be dug was turned into allotments. School playing fields, parks and tennis courts, all felt the spade. The king and queen even dug up the gardens of Buckingham Palace.

AND DRINK

Drink was seen as an enemy of the war effort. Once again the Royal Family set an example by giving up alchohol until the war was over. The Great War saw the start of limited drinking hours for pubs, which are still with us today.

Officially it was forbidden to eat crumpets, give bread to dogs, throw rice at weddings or stiffen your collar with starch (among other things), but actually, the rich could, and did, buy most things they wanted on the 'black market 👣 '.

Meanwhile, special advisers lectured the public on how to 'use as little food as you can' - which was pretty steep since many working class people were already underfed and had been long before the war started. Once rationing was introduced later in 1917, if anything, working people ate better than they'd done before because food was more fairly shared out.

👣 The 'black market' was for food and other items which were sold illegally.

The rations definitely helped. Before long there were rations for almost everything. Lloyd George, the 'New Conductor', had become Prime Minister in 1916. He ran Britain like a war machine. There were twelve different ration cards per person. It was even worse in Europe under the Central Powers. They had a joke about it:

... take a meat card, turn it in an egg card and fry it until nice and brown in a butter card. Cook the potato card and the vegetable card and add the flour card. After the meal one washes oneself with the soap card ...

A DOMESTIC SCENE
This soldier is glad to be back home in the bosom of his family. But someone is doing something they shouldn't. What is it?
(Answer on page 243.)

WHAT WOMEN DID

WE'RE RIGHT BEHIND YOU!

WORKERS, NOT SHIRKERS

Some people claim that men are more warlike than women, and perhaps they're right. But most women supported the Great War to the hilt. Many regretted that they didn't have the chance to fight and die like their men.

Before the war, most women didn't work outside the home. Just looking after the house was hard enough. There were few useful gadgets such as hoovers and washing machines to help out - and men weren't expected to help. Also, families tended to be large. Nine or ten children in a family wasn't uncommon. More children meant more work for their mothers.

Those women that did work outside the home tended to work in 'women's trades', for instance in the clothes industry or as house maids. The First World War changed all that. So many men were away fighting that large numbers of women were needed to do 'men's' jobs. By the end of the war five million women had full time jobs.

So many male farm workers went to war that farm land stood idle. Women's Land Army workers did all the jobs previously done by men. They wore men's clothes because they were more convenient.

Women drove motor cars on official business.

'Conductorettes' worked on trams and buses.

CANARIES

By the end of the war there were three times as many women as men working in the munitions factories of Britain. 'Munitionettes' worked twelve hour shifts building the guns and packing the explosive shells which flowed in a never-ending stream to the killing fields of France. The girls who worked with TNT, a high explosive, were known as 'canaries' because their faces turned a horrible yellow colour. They worked the 'monkey machines'. Four girls raised a heavy weight which was then dropped on to a mixture of TNT and amatol, packing it into the shell case. There were a lot of accidents.

MONEY, MONEY, MONEY

War meant money - for the workers back home at any rate. A British infantry man in France could be killed for just a shilling a day (5p, but worth more in those days); the girls in the factories could earn *forty shillings* a week. It wasn't fair, but it brought prosperity to many working class homes, especially since many of the older children worked as well. For the first time, many working class girls had money for luxuries. Munitionettes were always being scolded for their love of pretty clothes - and drink. Women's ready-made dress shops boomed while men's tailors went out of business by the bucketful - the men tended to die before they could pay their bills.

ARFA THIMBLE
GENTS TAILOR

War wasn't all bad. Life was short and people were desperate to enjoy it. Dancing was a major craze and the young women took full advantage. All kinds of dance clubs opened in London during the war, it was the same in Berlin and Paris. It was all the more intense as an experience because they never knew what might happen to their partners. A man might dance one day and die the next.

This was a time of growing freedom for women. Skirts were shorter due to the shortage of cloth, hair was shorter due to the danger of long hair getting stuck in machines, and wearing make-up and smoking in public became acceptable.

WAR FOR VOTES

Middle class women leapt at the chance which war gave them to escape the boredom of life stuck at home. In 1914 when the war started, voluntary women's committees in support of the war effort sprang up like dandelions in a cabbage patch. Khaki became a fashionable colour to wear (if you weren't in black for mourning).

As a reward for their support, women won the right to vote. Before the war, the suffragettes (the women who fought for the right to vote) were imprisoned, roughly handled by the police and force-fed when they went on hunger strike. In 1914 when the war started, women still couldn't vote. Despite this, most British suffragettes decided to throw their weight behind the war effort. As their leader Mrs Pankhurst put it: 'What would be the good of a vote without a country to vote in?'

Their gamble paid off. In 1918 when the war was over, women over thirty were given the right to vote. In 1928, this was extended to all women over twenty-one (the same as men).

INTO UNIFORM

More than 100,000 women joined the women's auxiliary services during the Great War. The first time ever that British women served in the armed forces:

WRNS, the Women's Royal Naval Service

WRAF, the Women's Royal Air Force

WAAC, the Women's Army Auxiliary Corps

The WAAC was the biggest service. *Les tommettes*, as the French called them suffered under petty rules, such as the one that said only officers could wear belts in their raincoats. Married women weren't allowed to serve in the same area as their husbands and barbed wire fences round WAAC camps kept men out and the women in.

The Great War also saw the first women police officers in Britain. Germany had them by 1905, but up until the war started, British policemen were still busy arresting women suffragettes so the idea of women police officers didn't make much sense. The very first English town to make use of women police was Grantham in Lincolnshire.

BLOOD AND GUTS

Toughest of all the volunteer services were the VADs, the Voluntary Aid Detachments. The VADs provided 15,000 nursing attendants and 23,000 nurses during the course of the war.

These young girls, often from sheltered middle and upper classes homes, helped men with the most ghastly wounds. They worked in hospitals near the front and lived mainly in tents. Winter was especially difficult. The tents froze rigid in the bitter cold - as did the women's clothes. They had to sleep in their clothes because it was impossible to put them on in the morning if they were frozen stiff.

Medicine came on in leaps and bounds during the war, but routine nursing was still a ghastly trade. Dressings on the worst wounds might have to be changed six times a day. At night the girls might go to bed stinking of pus. If that wasn't enough for them, they had to pick the lice from the uniforms of common soldiers.

AND GUTSY HEROES

The life of a VAD wasn't enough for everyone. Some women craved greater excitement.

Flora Sandes volunteered as a nurse, went to Serbia, served with a Serbian regiment, was wounded by hand grenades and ended up as a sergeant major in the Serbian army.

Mairi Chishholm and Mrs Knocker ran an unofficial first aid post immediately behind the front line. 'The two', as they became known, worked in terrifying conditions. They were frequently shelled and their drinking water, drained from the corpse-strewn ground, was green even after boiling. They treated all who came to them and were awarded the Star of the Order of Leopold II by the Belgian king.

FASHION VICTIM

Two mannequins from before and during the war have got muddled up. Which pieces should go with which? (Answer on page 243.)

LONG HAIR

SHORT HAIR

SMOKING

MAKE-UP

NO MAKE-UP

SHORT SKIRT

LONG SKIRT

BREAK-THROUGH!

THE END IS NIGH

TANKED UP

The way war was fought changed for ever in November 1917. Until then it was impossible for either side to attack without risking huge loss of life from machine gun fire. Tanks were armoured vehicles which protected men as they advanced, and November 1917 was when they were first used successfully. Their steel armour kept out everything except direct hits from artillery. Suddenly attack was no longer an especially unpleasant form of suicide.

But it was no thanks to the army that British soldiers were protected in this way. Given the danger of machine guns, you might think that army commanders would have fallen over themselves to find ways to protect their men during an attack. Well, forget it. Even Kitchener, and he was wiser than most, thought tanks were just mechanical toys. The development of the first tanks was left to the British *Admiralty*, which controls the *navy*, not the army. Winston Churchill, who was First Lord of the Admiralty in the early stages of the war, was almost the only top leader to see how useful tanks would be. The Germans never developed any good tanks until the next World War.

Early designs included a 'land battleship'. It was 30 metres long, 24 metres across and 14 metres high with massive naval guns, and it weighed 300 tons. It was carried on twelve-metre wheels. This huge beast wasn't practical and was never built.

Meanwhile, 'Little Willie' was born . Little Willie was the first proper tank. It had tracks which allowed it to travel across the roughest ground, although it never actually went into service.

Finding a name for the new weapon turned out to be quite a problem. They tried out 'land ship' and 'land cruiser', but felt that such names would give too much away to enemy spies. Without its tracks and guns the new weapon looked a bit like a 'cistern ' or a 'container'. Finally they settled on 'tank' because it meant much the same thing but was a shorter word.

The early tanks came in two sexes: male and female. Males had guns and females had machine guns. They worked together, the female giving supporting fire to the male.

Actually a similar and slightly better design had been suggested by a Mr Mole, an Australian, back in 1912, but no one had taken any notice.

A cistern is a place for storing water - like behind the toilet or in the loft.

Inside a tank

Early tanks were hell to drive. The inside was lit by a dim electric light, the temperature might rise as high as 120° and the guns were so noisy that they could split a man's eardrums. When machine gun bullets hit the outside, they set off an inferno of flying sparks inside. To protect themselves, the crew wore armour-plated masks, with slits for eye holes and chain-mail to cover their chins. They looked like something out of the middle ages.

Cambrai

Tanks were first tried out at the Battle of the Somme in 1916 but were a disappointment. They got bogged down in the mud and there weren't enough of them. This was Haig's fault. No credit to him that this failure turned out to be a blessing in disguise - the Germans decided that tanks were nothing to worry about.

In late 1917, General Haig had suffered yet another bloody set-back at the Third Battle of Ypres (see page 71). He needed a quick victory to 'restore his reputation'. So he decided to give the tank corps another chance.

The town of Cambrai  lay just behind German lines in an area of France which hadn't been fought over much, and so hadn't been churned into a sea of mud. It was excellent, firm rolling countryside - ideal for tanks.

The tanks were brought to Cambrai in strict secrecy. They were hidden beneath trees and in bombed-out buildings behind British lines.

The first thing the Germans heard on the morning of 20 November 1917, was the British guns followed by the roar of primitive engines. Then they saw 474 huge, dinosaur-like monsters roll out of the early morning mist towards them. The Germans fired their machine guns but the bullets just bounced off the monsters.

Where the word 'cambric' for a type of fabric comes from, due to the local industry of making fine fabrics.

The machines carried huge bundles of sticks which they dropped into the German trenches, then rolled over them.

In three days the tanks won 8 kilometres (5 miles) of land, Cambrai marked the end of the stalemate in France and the end of the reign of the evil machine gun.

BREAKTHROUGH!

As it turned out, Hindenburg and Ludendorff didn't mind too much about the bad news from Cambrai. They had good news from the east. On 6 November 1917, Bolshevik 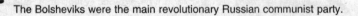 soldiers and sailors captured St Petersburg, the Russian capital. A new, Bolshevik government took power on the promise of 'no more war', and 6.5 million Russian troops on the eastern front stopped fighting. Germany was now free to move all her troops to the west to fight Britain and France. Hindenburg moved his headquarters nearer to the front line. He took plenty of books to read because, as he wrote to his wife: 'the days will be somewhat long'.

The Bolsheviks were the main revolutionary Russian communist party.

Ludendorff did all the work as usual. He planned to use his troops in small groups of 'storm troopers' backed up by rolling artillery fire.

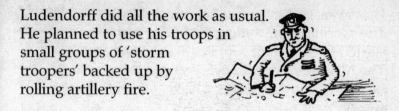

ROLLING ARTILLERY FIRE

Rolling artillery fire was used to back-up soldiers advancing towards the enemy on foot. As the soldiers moved forwards, shells from their own artillery were fired over their heads from behind them and were aimed to explode continuously about a hundred metres ahead of the soldiers as they advanced.

Hindenburg and Ludendorff wanted this attack to be the big one, the finishing blow against Britain and France. Before the German attack started they ordered the biggest artillery barrage the world has ever seen before or since. Then the Germans blasted their way forwards. By the end of May they'd fought to within 64 kilometres (40 miles) of Paris. It was the biggest breakthrough of the war so far.

However, Ludendorff's big attack ran out of steam. The German army moved too far, too fast and they started to run out of supplies of food and ammunition. The Allies fought them every step of the way and were helped by the Americans who had recently joined the war on their side.

THE YANKS ARE COMING!

When America had declared war on Germany in April 1917, most of the young soldiers didn't know what they were in for. They were given advice such as:

A complete bathing suit comes in handy.

Bring sneakers or slippers - they will add greatly to your comfort after a hard day's march.

Once they got to France they soon learned better.

A BLACK DAY

The German soldiers started to get seriously fed up. Would they ever be able to stop fighting? By July, the great German attack had fizzled out altogether, and on 18 July 1918 the Allied counter-attack began.

Due to the British blockade, the German troops were now down to a diet of dried turnips, horse meat and sawdust spread with a turnip paste known as 'Hindenburg fat'. Many of them lost all interest in fighting. Reports of German surrenders flooded back to German headquarters.

Then came 8 August 1918 - the 'Black Day' of the German army according to Ludendorff. 450 British tanks, backed up by British, Australian and Canadian soldiers captured 16,000 prisoners in a few hours near the old battlefield of the Somme. The Germans had crumbled like soggy biscuit.

LUDENDORFF LOSES IT

The strain of defeat was too much for Ludendorff. He took to drinking too much, crying suddenly and losing his temper for no reason. A doctor ordered rest, massage, no more talking in a high shrill voice of command, and the singing of German folk songs on waking. Amazingly, it worked - for a while.

But the bad news kept flooding in.

> 30 September 1918, Bulgaria caved in.
>
> 24 October - 2 November 1918, the Battle of
> Vittorio Veneto. Austria lost to the Italians. A
> quarter of a million Austrian deserters roamed
> the countryside, looting and pillaging.
>
> 27 October 1918, Austria caved in.

Hindenburg and Ludendorff couldn't cope any more.
They hid their heads in the sand like camels and tried
to pretend that it wasn't happening. They dreamed of
a peace treaty which would favour Germany. In their
dream treaty, Denmark and Holland would send back
all the German deserters  who had taken shelter
in their countries, and Germany would hang on to the
large chunks of eastern Europe which it had
conquered during the war.

The dream treaty was pie in the sky. Back in January,
President Woodrow Wilson of the USA had come up
with fourteen 'points' as the basis for peace. One of

Deserters are soldiers or sailors who have run away from the armed
forces. In time of war, deserters are often shot.

114

these points was that the Germans musn't hang on to any conquered land. Now the Allied peace terms became even tougher. They demanded that the Kaiser must give up his throne, and, worst of all, the Dreadful Duo themselves must go (in polite language of course).

It was awful - for the Dreadful Duo. On 27 October, the day Austria caved in, Ludendorff resigned after a row with the Kaiser. He then had a row with Hindenburg on the steps of the palace. The Duo was a duo no more.

Cinema audiences in Berlin cheered at the news that Ludendorff had resigned.

THE END

Germany itself was crumbling away. Riots broke out all over the place. If the leaders didn't make peace fast, they would have no country left to make peace with - and they couldn't make peace because the Allies refused peace as long as the Kaiser stayed on the throne.

At last, on 9 November, Kaiser Wilhelm gave up his throne. He boarded a special silver train and left for Holland, never to return. Germany and the world heaved a sigh of relief. Two days later, representatives of the German government met Marshal Foch, overall commander of the Allied armies in the west, in a train in the forest of Compiegne in northern France, to sign the armistice .

The war was over.

DEATH RIDE

Shortly before the armistice was signed, the admirals of the German navy decided on a 'death ride' - on 28 October, the German navy would sail forth to glorious defeat. But the German sailors weren't having any of it. They were sick and tired of their officers, who had feasted and held drinking bouts right through the war while their crews ate rubbish.

The sailors refused to weigh anchor. Those on ships already at sea put out the boilers. On a steam ship that means the ship can't move.

There was no death ride.

 Armistice means an agreement to end the fighting.

MEANWHILE, ELSEWHERE ...

This book has concentrated on the war in western Europe between Germany and France and Britain. But the War affected many other countries throughout the rest of the world.

AFRICA was a sideshow in the Great War. Quite small troops of soldiers, mainly African but with European officers, fought it out for control of Germany's few African colonies. Germany lost these colonies at the end of the war as a result of its defeat.

IRELAND was part of Britain in 1914. However, many Irish people wanted their own, independent Irish parliament. In 1916, some took matters into their own hands. The 'Easter Rising' was doomed to fail, but for a while the rebels took control of several buildings in central Dublin, including the central post office. When it was all over, the authorities ruthlessly executed the ringleaders.

The executions shocked the Irish and from then on they tended to become more anti-British. This left the Irishmen who had joined the British army high and dry. Many of them fought and died bravely, but they are sadly forgotten in their own country today.

ITALY was unsure whether or not to join the war in 1914. It joined the Allies in April 1915 and from then on spent the war fighting bravely against Austrian troops along the mountainous border between Italy and the Austro-Hungarian Empire.

RUSSIA lost around 1.8 million men during the Great War - about 12% of all who served in the army, although the war in the east was never quite as stuck in the mud as the war in France. During 1916, under General Brusilov, one of their few good commanders, the Russians fought back against Germany and especially against Austria, but they never really recovered from the defeat at Tannenberg at the start of the war. Russian soldiers were cursed by having too many foolish and proud commanders - a lot of them 'princes' with royal blood in their veins. It was small wonder that Russian soldiers formed the backbone of the Revolution which swept the Czar, the Russian Emperor, from power and took them out of the war in 1917.

TURKEY was known as 'the sick man' of Europe in 1914. By then the once-mighty Turkish Empire had already lost control of Greece, Serbia and Bulgaria. As a result of the war it lost control of the entire Arab world.

The Allies tried to invade Turkey via the peninsular of Gallipoli in 1915, but the Turks were brave soldiers and beat them off with heavy losses. Later in the war, the Turks lost to the British army and its Arab allies who fought northwards from their bases in Arabia and Egypt. The British forces were led by General Allenby and supported by the hero, Lawrence of Arabia, who wore Arab dress and helped the Arab fighters.

Turkey lost nearly a million men during the war - a higher percentage of its army than any other country, including France and Germany.

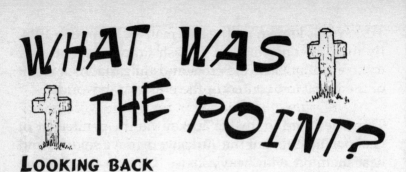

WHAT WAS THE POINT?

LOOKING BACK

WHAT A DIN!

The Great War ended at 11.00 am on 11 November 1918 - the eleventh hour of the eleventh day of the eleventh month.

When news of the armistice reached Britain, the whole country exploded with joy. Huge crowds gathered in the streets of London and other big cities. Boy scouts careered through the crowds on their bikes blowing the 'all clear' on their bugles, bells rang, the police blew their whistles. The party went on for three whole days.

Some of the returning soldiers found it hard to join in. Hiram Sturdy was in Glasgow. This is how he put it:

...singing, dancing, yelling people ... the pent-up feelings of four years of waiting, sorrow, loneliness, misery, wickedness, crimes and cruelty of unbelievable magnitude being sung, drunk and danced out.

FLU

As a reminder of the feebleness of people, even at their nastiest, compared to the power of nature, a flu epidemic swept round the world in the winter of 1918/19. Around *twenty-seven million* people are said to have died - *three times* the number who died because of the war - in just a few short months.

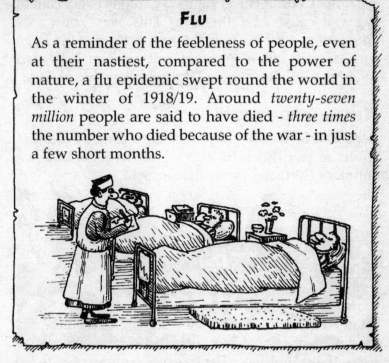

NO WAY TO TREAT AN ENEMY

On 28 June 1914, the war had started with the shooting of Archduke Franz Ferdinand in Sarejevo (see page 19). On 28 June 1919, exactly five years and about nine million dead soldiers later, the Treaty of Versailles was signed by defeated Germany.

Germany's nose was in the dirt and the Allies meant to keep it there. At the Treaty of Versailles, Germany and

A *treaty* is a signed agreement between two or more countries.

the other Central Powers agreed to repay every cent of damage caused by the war. This was known as 'reparations' and the final figure was fixed at the huge sum of £6.6 billion plus interest (add at least two noughts for today's value), payable over thirty years.

WHAT HAPPENED NEXT

Reparations were so enormous that Germany couldn't afford to pay them. In 1923 France took control of a chunk of Germany for a while instead.

In 1925 Hindenburg, who should have been retired, was elected president of Germany - and again in 1932. The next year, he chose as his chancellor (like our Prime Minister) another old soldier of the Great War. That soldier's name was Adolf Hitler, now leader of the National Socialist Party of Germany - 'Nazis' for short. Hitler, like many Germans, was still bitter about losing the First World War and about the cost of reparations. Six years later, in 1939, he led the Germans into the Second World War.

It's hard to find anything good to say about the First World War. It did however change the world forever.

In Britain, in the 'Khaki' election which followed victory, Lloyd George (the British Prime Minister) promised a 'land fit for heroes'. It was never a land fit for heroes but there were some changes:

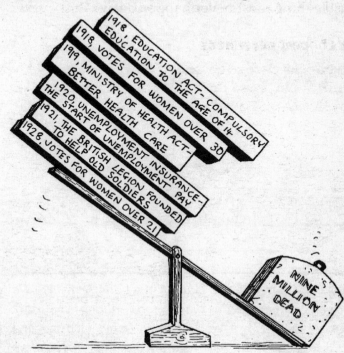

1918, EDUCATION ACT- COMPULSORY EDUCATION TO THE AGE OF 14

1918, VOTES FOR WOMEN OVER 30

1919, MINISTRY OF HEALTH ACT- BETTER HEALTH CARE

1920, UNEMPLOYMENT INSURANCE- THE START OF UNEMPLOYMENT PAY

1921, THE BRITISH LEGION FOUNDED -TO HELP OLD SOLDIERS

1928, VOTES FOR WOMEN OVER 21

NINE MILLION DEAD

RED IS FOR REMEMBRANCE

We still live with the First World War. In every town and every village across Europe there's a war memorial with a long, sad list of the dead and in France and Belgium the cemeteries of the war dead go on for miles.

In Britain every year when autumn comes around, we wear red paper poppies in memory of the killing fields of France. And on the eleventh hour of the eleventh day of the eleventh month, when the war ended, we all stand silently for two minutes to show our respect for the dead, and our determination that such a terrible thing must never happen again.

Let's hope it never does.

end of World War I

Hello, my name's Linda Hand. I'm a Land Army girl. We helped farmers to produce food during the dark dangerous days of World War II. Come with me and we'll find out what war meant for ordinary people, as well as for the generals and politicians.

DOODLE-BUG!

BEWARE BUZZ-BOMBS.

First of all, let's find out what life was like on the street.

MUMBLE MUMBLE... GRUMBLE?

ARTHUR CAB...

ONE QUIET AFTERNOON ...

London, August 1944. Two women step out of a greengrocer's shop with bags of shopping and their hair in curlers, their clothes clean but shabby. A workman climbs out of a hole in the road where he's been working. No one's in a rush, and all seems peaceful as a snooze in the park.

There's just a bit of a noise in the sky above. It sounds something like a cheap motorbike in need of a service.

Nobody seems to take any notice.

Then the motorbike-noise cuts out. The two women calmly step back into the grocer's shop and the workman slips back into his hole.

Next moment there's a rush of wind and a loud bomb-explosion somewhere close, followed by the clatter of bricks and glass on tarmac. Then the two women come out of the grocer's, still chatting, and the workman pops out of his hole. Life goes on.

Bombs were frightening. But in the summer of 1944 the brave people who stayed in London had learned to put up with them.

Buzz off!

The bomb with the noisy engine was called a V1 flying bomb, also known as a 'doodle-bug' or 'buzz-bomb'. They flew at about 640 kph, but it was only when the engine stopped that you had to worry. No engine noise meant that a V1 was about to plunge to earth. It wasn't a good idea to be underneath when it did.

Doodle-bugs were designed to cause maximum havoc. Like all bombs, they killed and wounded people and destroyed their homes.

World War II had been going on for five years by the summer of 1944, and millions of people all over the world had died because of it. The British had got used to living in fear of death during bombing campaigns. And as well as bombs they had got used to a lot of other things, like not having much food for instance, or having to patch up their old clothes.

War had become a way of life.

But at least by 1944 they were winning - it wasn't like that at first.

BULLY FOR YOU!

OR - WHO STARTED IT?

Germany lost World War I in 1918. Millions had died. It was called the 'war that will end war'. Britain, France and Russia had been Germany's main enemies.

WELL, THAT SHOULD DO IT.

I'VE HAD ENOUGH OF THIS!

FANCY ANOTHER ONE?

World War II started just twenty-one years after the end of World War I and it was even bigger. It spread out from Europe like a cancer until most of the world was fighting. On one side were Britain, France, the countries of the British Empire, and other allies of the British. (The Americans joined the British later.) On the other side were Germany, Japan, and Italy and their allies. The German side were called the 'Axis Powers', the British side were called the 'Allies'.

Allies are a bit like friends. Countries which are *allied* to each other will fight on the same side during a war.

HOW IT ALL BEGAN

Back in 1939 when World War II started, Britain was a world super-power - just as America is today, but more so in some ways. The British Empire included India, Pakistan, half of Africa, Australia, New Zealand, Canada, Hong Kong and Singapore, plus other countries.

Britain was rich and powerful, but her army was quite small and out-of-date. Greedy eyes were watching her.

THE BRITISH EMPIRE

THE AMERICANS WANTED TO CUT HER DOWN TO SIZE.

THE JAPANESE WANTED AN EMPIRE OF THEIR OWN IN THE EAST.

THE GERMANS WANTED TO BE THE MOST POWERFUL NATION IN THE WORLD.

THE ITALIANS WANTED TO START ANOTHER ROMAN EMPIRE.

THE RUSSIANS WANTED BITS OF BRITAIN'S EMPIRE IN THE EAST.

POOR OLD GERMANS

It was the Germans who were the biggest problem.

After the German defeat at the end of the First World War the German Ruhr region had been run by the French.

Millions of Germans lived in land governed by Poles, Czechs or Russians.

In the 1920s German money lost its value, causing great suffering. You needed so much money to buy the simplest things that people would sometimes take their money to the shop in a wheelbarrow.

Millions of workers around the world had become unemployed during the Great Depression in the 1930s. Germans suffered more than most.

In 1933 the Germans found a new leader who they hoped would solve their problems. His name was Adolf Hitler.

ADOLF SCHICKELGRUBER - NEVER HEARD OF HIM!

In 1876 a small-time Austrian customs official called Schickelgruber changed his name to Hitler. Then in 1889 he and his wife had a baby son whom they called Adolf. No one could have guessed that this baby would grow up to be one of the most evil men who has ever lived.

Young Adolf wanted to be a great artist, but he wasn't good enough. Unfortunately he had another hobby - politics. In 1919, having moved to Germany, he became the seventh member of the tiny National Socialist German Workers' Party - or Nazis for short. From then on politics stopped being a hobby and became a way of life.

There was no stopping him. He turned out to be a political genius, becoming first leader of the Nazi Party and then, in 1933, Chancellor of all Germany, by which time his Nazi Party had thousands of members.

The world was going to have to take notice of Adolf Schickelgruber/Hitler.

The German *Chancellor* does the same sort of job as the British Prime Minister.

WHICH IS THE REAL HITLER?

Adolf Hitler was a very evil man. Like many evil men he could seem kind and jolly to his friends and family if he wanted to. In fact, like many dangerous men, he would never have been able to cause as much suffering as he did, if a lot of people hadn't been fooled by him.

VEGETARIAN.

LOVES CHILDREN.

LIKES PAINTING WATERCOLOURS.

RACIST.

LOVES POWER.

BAD IDEAS

Hitler's Party came to power with some dangerous ideas which were bound to cause trouble. Here are some of them:

Unfortunately Hitler seemed to sort out the German economy in no time. He started a massive programme to build guns, warships, planes and tanks, which meant that most men had a job, for a while. He introduced a housing scheme, motorways, equal pay for women, and better family allowances. He promised that everyone would have a house of their own and a car. Many Germans felt better off than at any time since World War I.

Although many Germans felt better off, a lot of them didn't but kept quiet about it.

Even before gaining power the Nazis had learned how to frighten people who disagreed with them. They staged huge, terrifying, political demonstrations and attacked their enemies on the streets.

Soon only a few very brave people dared to stand up to them.

THE MASTER RACE

The Nazis believed that Germans, or rather *Aryans* (a word which included some other north-Europeans), were the *Master Race*. Members of the Master Race were meant to have fair hair and blue eyes if possible. It was their duty to rule the world. And their empire would last a thousand years.

The Nazis realised that there weren't enough members of the Master Race to rule everywhere immediately, so the first duty of German women was to have lots of children. Women who left work to marry were paid special marriage vouchers worth an average eight months' wages. They might be awarded the 'Mothers' Cross' if they had a lot of children. Divorce, birth-control, abortion and homosexuality were all made illegal because they stopped women from having as many babies as possible. Soon there were lots of blue-eyed babies.

From the very beginning the Nazis wanted Germany to be 'racially pure'. There was no room in their

Germany for Jews or gypsies or anyone who opposed them. So all these other people were allowed to have as many divorces and abortions as they wanted. But of course legal abortions and divorce wouldn't altogether stop these people having children: huge prisons or 'concentration camps' for unwanted people were bound to result from Nazi ideas.

So what about other countries? Well other races were meant to serve the Master Race. Once the Germans ruled the world these other races would be specially bred to make good servants and workers.

It all sounds like madness now. As Hitler's right-hand man, Joseph Goebbels, admitted at the time: *'If the German people had known what the Nazi Party intended to do once it gained power, they would never have voted for it'.*

But fortunately for the Nazis, and unfortunately for the rest of the world, the Germans didn't know what the Nazi Party intended - and a lot of them *did* vote for it - as long as Hitler let them vote.

Hitler had become Chancellor in 1932 after winning an election. By the summer of 1933 he had crushed all the opposition political parties. And in 1934 he became both Chancellor and President of Germany at the same time. From then on he became known as the *Reichs Chancellor* or *Fuhrer*, which means 'leader'. There would be no more elections to the German *Reichstag*, or parliament, as long as the *Fuhrer* was in power.

FASCIST FACTS

The German Nazis were fascists. In a fascist state people are meant to obey their rulers without question. Those who disobey are punished ruthlessly, and there's no voting for a change of government.

Fascists are extreme nationalists, meaning they want their own country to have as much power as possible, normally at the expense of other countries. They usually hate people of other races, especially if people of other races share their country with them.

The first fascist party was started in 1919 in Italy. Its leader was a blacksmith's son called Benito Mussolini.

Mussolini

The Italian fascists planned to build a new Roman Empire, and the word *fascist* comes from the Latin word *fasces* for the bundles of rods with an axe sticking out which were carried on ancient Roman state processions. Italian fascist thugs were known as 'black-shirts' from their uniform.

GRUESOME GALLERY

A noxious nest of nasty Nazis.

 GOEBBELS

Dr Joseph Goebbels was in charge of all Nazi publicity. As editor of the newspaper *Der Angriff*, he whipped up hatred of Jews and Communists. He and his wife killed themselves and their six children in 1945.

GOERING

An ex-World War I fighter-pilot and art-lover who looted the museums of Europe of their treasures, Hermann Goering was head of the German air force and became for a while the second most powerful Nazi after Hitler. He poisoned himself in 1946, on the eve of his execution.

HEYDRICH

Reinhard Heydrich was head of the German security services and hideously cruel. He wrote the first draft of *The Final Solution to the Jewish Problem* which argued for the mass-murder of Jews.

 SPEER

Albert Speer was an architect turned Nazi who rose to control German industry during the War. He was sentenced to twenty years in prison after the War for his use of slave labour.

STREICHER

A vicious Nazi hate-monger, Julius Streicher staged the massive Nuremberg Rallies. Found guilty of corruption, he retired to his farm in 1940. He was executed for war crimes in 1946.

OLYMPIC GAMES STORY

In August 1936 the Olympic Games were held in Berlin, the capital of Germany. Here was a great opportunity to prove to the world that the Master Race were best at athletics. The stadium held a massive 110,000 crowd from all over the world.

Unfortunately for the Nazis, the star of the games was Jesse Owens, who won the gold medals for the hundred metres and the two hundred metres. Jesse was a black American - nothing like a member of the Master Race!

Hitler was very angry to see Jesse beat his German athletes - so angry that during the medal awards ceremony he refused to shake Jesse's hand and then left the stadium.

THOUSAND-YEAR REICH

The Nazis called their hoped-for empire the Thousand-Year Reich. They planned to have colonies of conquered people working for them all over the world, and they planned how they would rule them. During the Second World War, whenever they conquered a new country they put their ideas into practice.

 Jews and other 'undesirables', such as gypsies, homosexuals and communists, were sent to concentration camps to be worked to death.

 Able-bodied men from Eastern Europe were used as slave labour in German factories (the *Volkswagen* company used lots of slave labour).

 Conquered lands were ruled by provincial governors who were as powerful as little kings in their own areas. The provincial governors were very brutal Nazis. They made many extra enemies for the Germans.

SS - SERIOUSLY SINISTER

To make sure the provincial governors obeyed orders from Germany they were watched by a special force of Nazis known as the *SS* 🔫 . These were meant to be the cream of the Master Race. It was said that they were so perfect that even if a man had a filling in his tooth he couldn't join them.

Hitler planned that the SS would be the power-house of his new empire. They were trained to be completely ruthless in enforcing Nazi ideas. So if an SS man was in command of a concentration camp he could be

---

SS stands for *Schutzstaffel*, meaning 'protection squadron'.

horribly brutal to the prisoners without feeling bad about it. After all, according to Nazi ideas, by killing prisoners he was helping to 'cleanse' Germany of her enemies.

SPACE RACE

Hitler wanted to breed more members of the Master Race to run his empire, but at the same time he believed there wasn't enough land in Germany for members of the Master Race already living in it. He thought they needed living space.

The first task was to gather all Germans together into one country.

March 1936. German troops march into the Rhineland in Southern Germany, forbidden to them since World War I.

March 1938. Austria, which has a population of over six million German-speakers, taken over by Germany in an operation known as the Anschluss.

September 1938. At a meeting in Munich, the British Prime Minister, Neville Chamberlain, agrees that Germany can take over the Sudetenland in Czechoslovakia, home to three million Germans.

IT IS PEACE IN OUR TIME.

The next task was to grab more living space. Hitler wanted to take it from Eastern Europe.

March 1939. German troops invade the rest of Czechoslovakia. Britain and France do not interfere.

In **September 1939** German troops (and their Russian allies) attack Poland. But this time Hitler has gone too far. After all, who might he invade next? France and Britain declare war on Germany.

World War II has begun - only twenty-one years after World War I has ended. Ordinary Germans are no happier about it than the British or French.

WHAT'S ALL THE FUSS ABOUT?

THE PHONEY WAR.

As soon as it had declared war on Germany, the British Parliament passed a law saying that all men between the ages of eighteen and forty-one had to join the army, navy or air force if they were asked to.

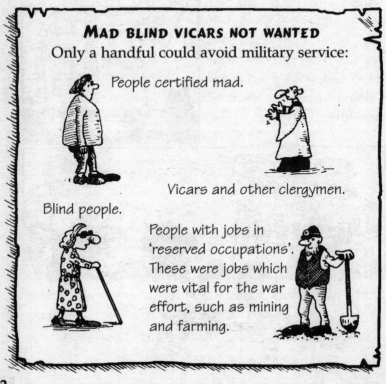

MAD BLIND VICARS NOT WANTED
Only a handful could avoid military service:

People certified mad.

Vicars and other clergymen.

Blind people.

People with jobs in 'reserved occupations'. These were jobs which were vital for the war effort, such as mining and farming.

A small number of men were pacifists. This meant that they didn't believe in war, even against the evil of the Nazis.  These people were called 'conscientious objectors'. They still had to join the armed services if they were asked, but in non-fighting jobs such as ambulance driver.

ALL RIGHT TOM?

Men flocked to join the army. Between May and December 1939, 761,600 men and 31,960 women joined up. Most of them had never been soldiers before - and would never want to be soldiers again once the War was over.

New 'Tommies', as British soldiers were called, got a short haircut, a new uniform (which was rough and itchy till you got used to it) and fourteen weeks' training, which mainly involved marching around and learning to shoot their weapons. Here are some of them:

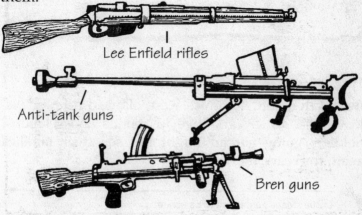

Lee Enfield rifles

Anti-tank guns

Bren guns

Then, with their new weapons and uniforms, the soldiers were packed off to France to wait for the Germans.

MAD MOBILE MINE

Throughout the War rival armies raced to invent new and more deadly weapons. In 1940 King Haakon VII of Norway was chased across Roehampton golf links by a demonstration 'mobile mine' which had run out of control. He was saved when its wheels got stuck in a bunker!

IT'S NO HOLIDAY

Before they left, Tommies were allowed a few days' leave 🦶 to say goodbye to friends and relations. Soldiers going abroad might not see their families again for years, if ever.

🦶 *Leave* means permission to be absent.

144

For those who went abroad, everything seemed very different from England. It was the first time most of them had been away and they weren't ready for it. As one soldier said of the French:

'They have eggs but they don't fry them properly, they cook them. Bread they give you in big chunks. Tea they cannot make at all, and I didn't like the coffee.'

Once abroad their only contact with home was by post. Letters from home were more precious than gold. The Government understood how important letters were, and it made sure that postage from England took only about three days, even in battle conditions. The army postmen worked hard: during Christmas 1939 they delivered vast quantities of parcels and letters.

Letters were censored in case enemy spies got hold of them - meaning that the letters were read by an officer to make sure they didn't give away any secrets. Tommies could send an uncensored 'Field Service Postcard', but all that said was the date, address and name of sender to show he was still alive.

When the Tommies got to France there was nothing much to do at first. Fortunately the army believed in keeping its soldiers fit and healthy: each battalion had fifty kilograms of sports gear, including twenty-four hockey sticks, fifty pairs of football boots and strip enough for six teams.

DOWN ON THE FARM

At the same time as the army of Tommies was leaving for France, another army was leaving home - for the countryside. This army was mostly made up of children who were evacuated  from their homes in the big cities in case of German bomb attacks.

THE OTHER ARMY

In the first big evacuation in 1939 these were evacuated:

12,000 pregnant women.

103,000 teachers and helpers.

827,000 schoolchildren.

524,000 toddlers with their mothers.

+ 7,000 disabled people.

Evacuation meant being sent away from home to somewhere safer.

Some dogs were evacuated too. One advertisement read:

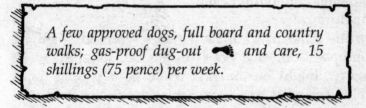

A few approved dogs, full board and country walks; gas-proof dug-out *and care, 15 shillings (75 pence) per week.*

Sometimes the children wore name-labels on their clothes. When they arrived, people chose which children they wanted to stay with them. It could be a bit like an auction. In other places everything was well-organised in advance.

Sometimes children from well-off families stayed in poor country cottages, and sometimes poor children stayed in large country mansions. If the children came

A *dug-out* was an underground air-raid shelter.

from poor town families, they might never have seen a cow or a sheep before and would have come from miserable conditions at home.

On the other hand, if the families who took them in were well-off, the poor 'evacuees', as they were known, might be the first really poor people these well-off families had ever seen at close quarters. There was a huge gap between the upper and lower classes in those days.

Some of the evacuees had always slept under their parents' bed and they refused to sleep in a proper bed because they weren't used to it.

Many didn't know how to use a toothbrush.

Many of the children's heads were crawling with head lice.

As the Prime Minister said in a letter: '*I never knew such conditions existed, and I feel ashamed of having been so ignorant of my neighbours*'.

Many of the children had a great time in the countryside and loved the comfy cottage beds and playing in the fields. But some of them felt terribly homesick as soon as they arrived. One wrote home on a postcard: *'Dear Mum, I hope you are well. I don't like the man's face much. Perhaps it will look better in the daylight. I like the dog's face best.'*

It wasn't just people who were evacuated.

The Bank of England was evacuated to the village of Overton in Hampshire.

The paintings of the National Gallery were moved to a slate quarry in Wales.

Aliens beware!

Everyone was given a gas mask and expected to carry it with them all the time, in case German planes dropped poison-gas bombs. Gas masks had a snout to breathe through and two eye-holes. When people put them on they looked like aliens from outer space. There were even special gas-proof cots for babies.

So where's the war then?

So there were all the British - many of them in the armed forces or living with strangers in the countryside, most of them lugging their gas masks around everywhere.

And nothing happened.

Hitler just couldn't make up his mind when to attack. Summer turned to autumn, and autumn to winter. This strange time when nothing happened was called the 'Phoney War'.

That winter of 1939 the British soldiers in France settled down as best they could in odd places such as barns and stables. Many slept on straw. Back in England people stopped carrying their gas masks and the evacuated children drifted back to their homes in the cities.

By the following April the Prime Minister felt able to announce *'Hitler has missed the bus!'* After all, nothing was happening.

Or was it ...?

DAD'S ARMY

WE SHALL FIGHT THEM WITH FORKS –
IF WE HAVE TO.

A week later, on 9 April 1940, German armies smashed through Denmark and invaded Norway.

British troops rushed to defend Norway, but were driven off.

WAR ON WHEELS

It was as easy as squashing flies. The German army was the best in Europe. They'd had plenty of practice invading Czechoslovakia and Poland. They were tough soldiers and they moved as quick as lightning.

In fact lightning, or *Blitzkrieg* (meaning 'lightning-war'), was the word they used to describe their tactics. You see, the Germans were the first people to realise that aircraft used with tanks and lorries made war happen much faster than in the past. Everyone else attacked at about the speed of their poor old foot-soldiers, but the Germans barged ahead in tanks, while their special *Stuka* dive-bombers swooped down on the enemy from above. It worked only too well.

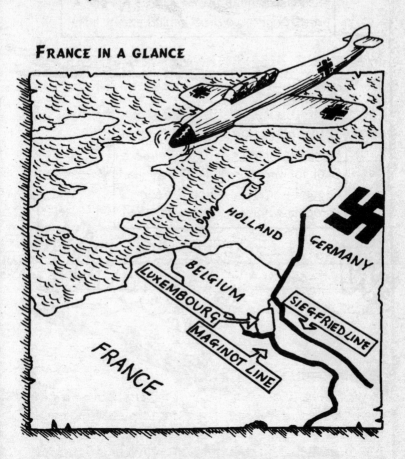

FRANCE IN A GLANCE

Having gobbled up Norway and Denmark, it was time for the Germans to take a bite at France. The French had built a massive great defence system, called the 'Maginot Line', along their border with Germany, but the Germans simply drove round it, attacking through Belgium on 10 May 1940. Their Blitzkrieg tactics were just as successful against the French and the British as they were against everyone else ...

Their aeroplanes towed gliders full of paratroopers to drop behind enemy lines.

Their screeching Stukas dive-bombed helpless foot-soldiers. Stukas were terrifying. They had special sirens which made a screaming noise as they attacked.

They dropped dummy paratroopers to frighten the enemy into thinking there were more of them than there really were.

WWOOOW

Their tanks drove in huge herds which crushed all opposition.

In next to no time half of France was occupied by the Germans, and the other half, to be known as 'Vichy France', was ruled by a government which was friendly towards Germany. The French and the British armies were forced back to the English Channel. It looked as if they would have no choice except to drown in the sea or surrender.

But Britain had a secret weapon ...

WINNIE THE POOH!

Winston Churchill, or 'Winnie' for short, loved smoking big, fat, smelly cigars and drank whisky all day. He liked a fight.

After the invasion of Norway, Neville Chamberlain resigned as Prime Minister. He had cancer but also people blamed him for not standing up to the Nazis when the Nazis invaded Czechoslovakia. Winnie took over. He was just what Britain needed.

One thing Winston Churchill would never do was surrender.

RETREAT!

Back in Europe, in June 1940, the British and French armies retreated into a narrow strip of land around the French port of Dunkirk. All the ships available in Britain were sent across the British Channel to carry the troops back to England. There were big warships, cross-channel ferries, even paddle-steamers.

But the big ships couldn't get in close enough to shore for the soldiers to wade out to them. Inspired by Winnie, the call went out for smaller boats to sail across. Soon the Channel was dotted with a vast number of small boats, like a mad yachting regatta.

In a blazing hell of dive-bombers and gun-fire the British ships saved nearly 340,000 men - most of the British army and more than a hundred thousand French soldiers.

It was an amazing escape, but on the other hand the British had suffered sixty-eight thousand casualties.

Once back in England the British soldiers were exhausted but safe. As one said: *'I've had no sleep for a week. I could sleep on a clothes line.'* They were greeted with sandwiches and cups of tea. And their escape had been so amazing and lucky that they were treated more like conquering heroes than a defeated army.

Just one thing was wrong ...

They had left behind 90,000 rifles, 64,000 vehicles, 50,800 tonnes of ammunition and stores, as well as many guns. It was only a matter of time before the Germans would try to invade Britain, and Britain had very few weapons left to fight them off.

BELL-RINGING GERMAN GLIDER-PILOT WITH PARACHUTE NEEDED TO REPLACE MISSING SIGNPOSTS

Hardly anyone thought of making peace with the Germans, in spite of Dunkirk. They were encouraged by Winnie, who made a famous speech saying that this was their 'finest hour'. In fact the British felt surprisingly good.

Already many preparations had been made in case of a German invasion, and now everybody worked harder than ever.

All signposts were taken down so that the enemy army would get lost - this probably caused more problems for the British than it would have done for the Germans.

IT DOESN'T LOOK MUCH LIKE BIRMINGHAM TO ME, CORPORAL!

Pillboxes were built where it would be easiest to hold up an advancing army, for instance beside bridges. Pillboxes were strong concrete or brick shelters built to protect guns from enemy fire.

Large fields were planted with poles and wire to stop gliders landing.

Railway station signs were taken down. You had to ask people where you were.

Bell-ringing was forbidden except as a warning that German paratroopers had arrived.

At last - Dad's Army

To help the regular army, in May 1940 the Government had asked for men aged anywhere between seventeen and sixty-five to report to their local police station and join a new 'Home Guard'.

Men rummaged in dusty cupboards and sheds and grabbed what weapons they could, from old shotguns and World War I rifles to the odd garden fork. Then they marched down to the local police station. So many rushed to join that in one village in Kent the policeman thought he was facing a mob of armed rioters rather than a crowd of law-abiding volunteers. By July the Home Guard had grown to a million and a half members.

Pretty well anyone was welcome. The oldest was in his eighties. There was no medical examination to make sure they were fit. All that was asked was that they had 'free movement', whatever that meant. No one had to have any experience of firing a rifle, although many of them had fought in World War I. In fact, in the early days there weren't that many rifles to fire. They were so short of weapons that at one stage some were given pikes  made of an iron tube with a knife blade on the end.

SEVEN THOUSAND AND THIRTY-ONE, SEVEN THOUSAND AND THIRTY-TWO...

In July the Home Guard was given 500,000 World War I rifles from America. These had been kept in thick sticky oil since 1918 to stop them going rusty. The job of cleaning them was almost enough to make you want to surrender to the Germans. Just cleaning eight thousand took two hundred and fifty women a fortnight's hard work.

COW OR SEA LION?

It's hard to believe that the Home Guard could have stood up to the Germans for long. They were badly-armed and nervous. Several cows were shot in the dark by members of the Home Guard who thought the cows were German paratroopers.

Pikes are a medieval weapon. They are a very long pole with a blade, spike or axe on the end and were very useful against armoured knights on horseback.

And the Germans were gathering barges for the invasion. They had their plan all worked out. It was called *Operation Sea Lion*. The day after their invasion was to be called *S Day*. They were going to attack along the south coast of England and hoped to mop up the whole country in a week or two.

There was just one problem - they had to take control of the skies to stop the British bombing their barges when they crossed the Channel ...

BLACK AS A PIECE OF COAL IN A BLACK BAG

LOST BOMBER SEEKS SPECK OF LIGHT FOR HOMEWARD JOURNEY.

The summer of 1940 was fabulous. One lovely, long, hot, sunny day followed another. England looked beautiful, and although there were some German bomber attacks, it was hard to believe they would ever amount to much. Crowds of sightseers came to see the damage, and little children clambered around the bomb-craters looking for bits of bomb, called shrapnel, to keep.

In 1941 one girl found a German airman's glove in a bomb-crater. She took it home to show to her mum. But when she put it on the kitchen table - she found it had a hand inside it!

Everything looked as peaceful as a cat in a hammock, but in the clear blue sky over southern England a deadly battle was about to start. Goering, the head of the German *Luftwaffe* , had persuaded Hitler that he could win control of the air before the main German invasion started. The first big attack was fixed for 13 August, which was called *Adlertag*, or Eagle Day.

The Battle of Britain had begun.

The *Luftwaffe* (meaning 'Air Weapon') was the German air force.

PILOT PROBLEMS

During the Battle of Britain, the British had too few planes and too few pilots to fly them.

Factories churned out new planes as fast as possible, and people gave money to help build them. Through the Spitfire Fund you could 'buy' a bit of a plane - for instance sixpence for a rivet, twenty-two pounds for a small bomb.

Meanwhile the handful of pilots had to keep flying almost round the clock. As the weeks passed and the battle in the air dragged on, the pilots became exhausted. *'You were too tired even to get drunk,'* as one of them said. They often took off with new wounds quickly bandaged. One young pilot used to be sick every time on his way to the plane, because, in the words of another young pilot: *'Most of us were pretty scared all the bloody time.'*

Then after a few weeks the German pilots were ordered to bomb British cities. This meant that they had little time left over to damage British airfields and planes on the ground. The British could rebuild and repair their air force between battles in the air.

The Germans had made a big mistake. By September 1940 it was clear that they would not be able to destroy the Royal Air Force. The Battle of Britain was over.

BALLOON BATTLE

Cables from barrage balloons were designed to get tangled up in enemy aircraft. You are an enemy bomber. Can you find your way to safety through the British barrage balloons?

EXPECT THE WORST

The Battle of Britain was over, but the bombing of Britain had only just begun. Many German bombers got past the British planes and dropped their bombs on the cities of Britain. In September the Germans started night bombing raids and this went on for the rest of the *Blitz*, as the German bombing was called.

Before the War it was calculated that the Luftwaffe could drop 700,000 kilograms of bombs per day on London. So the Government had expected the worst and planned for it:

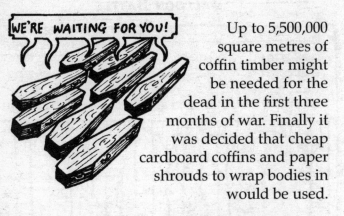

Up to 5,500,000 square metres of coffin timber might be needed for the dead in the first three months of war. Finally it was decided that cheap cardboard coffins and paper shrouds to wrap bodies in would be used.

There might be 4,000,000 mental cases in the first six months, as well as all the other casualties.

As it turned out, things weren't quite that bad. But they were still pretty awful ...

BOMBED TO BLITZ

The first warning of a bombing raid was the wail of the air-raid sirens, followed by the drone of the bombers' engines. Then powerful searchlights pierced the night sky and the anti-aircraft guns started up.

In fact more British civilians than German airmen were killed by anti-aircraft shell-fragments, and one local council said that the vibrations of the guns damaged the toilet bowls in their council houses. But on the other hand, the anti-aircraft guns forced the bombers to fly high, so that they couldn't aim their bombs so well.

In the first stage of the Blitz, up till November, 10,000 people were killed. Which is a lot, but not as many as the Government had expected. The biggest problem turned out to be where to put all the newly-homeless people after their houses were bombed. These bombed-out people were always covered in dirt and dust and were often in their night-clothes. Only a few rest centres were ready for them. Rest centres never had enough places to wash and there was often only bread and margarine to eat.

Fire-bombs or 'incendiaries' caused some of the worst damage. If a fire-bomb fell on a warehouse the result could be spectacular. There were rubber fires producing clouds of dangerous smoke, rum fires (which smelt lovely), and even pepper fires which made your eyes water. During one blaze it was possible to read a newspaper in Shaftesbury Avenue in London by the light of flames five miles away.

> Sometimes the rats would be driven from their nests and thousands of them would run through the streets.

ORDINARY HEROES

Some of the bravest people in the War weren't in the armed forces at all.

 Firemen often fought fires while bombs fell around them.

 Fire watchers, armed only with a stirrup pump and a water bucket, put out many small fires before they could blaze up.

 ARP (stands for Air Raid Precautions) wardens each controlled an area of about five hundred people. Mostly they were part-time.

SHELTERING FROM THE BLAST

Most of Britain's major cities were badly bombed, but London got the worst of it. When the air-raid siren sounded, everyone rushed for shelter.

They might take refuge in an 'Anderson Shelter'. In the garden a pit was dug and covered by a curved roof made from fourteen sheets of corrugated steel. Then earth was piled on top. Vegetables were often planted on the roof.

Other people stayed indoors in a 'Morrison Shelter'. This was a large box with a steel roof. It could stand up to the collapse of a two-storey house.

Advice for dog owners: *'When you take him in the shelter, put him on a lead. If you can put a muzzle on him you should do so because he may get hysterical during the raids. Put some cotton-wool in his ears.'*

Designed by Dr David Anderson, production and distribution organised by Home Secretary, Sir John Anderson.

Named after Herbert Morrison, Minister of Home Security.

Eighty London underground stations were used as air-raid shelters at night. Some people would queue all day for a place on the platform for their families. Library services were provided, and a few stations were fitted out with bunk-beds. But underground stations were uncomfortable. They were a breeding ground for lice, and deep under ground, below the level of main sewage drains, there were no toilets because at that depth there were no drains beneath the stations for the toilets to drain into.

YOU'LL JUST HAVE TO WAIT TILL MORNING.

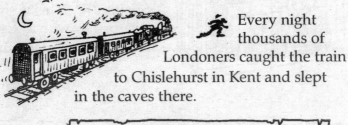

Every night thousands of Londoners caught the train to Chislehurst in Kent and slept in the caves there.

CLEAR OFF, ROVER!

Dogs were forbidden in public air-raid shelters.

There were shelters in the basements of some very strong buildings.

BANK OF ENGLAND

Trench shelters were dug in public squares.

The Germans also had air-raid shelters. Some of the Berlin shelters were huge. The one under Berlin Zoo could sleep ten thousand.

ROOM FOR ONE MORE?

ACHTUNG!

SPOT THE SPY

The animals have taken over the shelter beneath Berlin Zoo. One is a British spy - but which is it?

Answer: The one with the briefcase.

Every night everyone in Britain suffered from black out. This didn't mean that they became unconsciou the idea of the black-out was to stop Germa bombers from seeing the lights of towns and village Every light had to be covered up:

Night-trains had their blinds drawn, with only a blue pinpoint of light on the ceiling in each compartment. They were really gloomy.

Black-out curtains were fastened to all windows.

Traffic lights were fitted with hoods on top and black shields showing only a small cross of light at the front for each colour.

Torches had to be covered with two layers of tissue paper.

Train and bus windows were covered against flying glass, with just a small slit to let passengers see the name of the station or bus-stop. The buses were so dark inside that bus conductors had a hard job seeing what money they were given. Many dud coins were handed over.

One good thing came of it all: for the first time in more than a hundred years the stars could be seen shining clearly over London and other big cities.

And one bad thing came of it: the number of road accidents more than doubled. Car headlights were covered. Only a tiny slit was left uncovered to shine light down onto the road.

The Germans had a black-out too. Keen Nazis wore luminous buttons in the shape of the *swastika* .

The *swastika* was the symbol of the Nazis. It's based on an ancient Hindu sign meaning 'well-being'.

ALL CLEAR!

Germany had lost the Battle of Britain by September 1940, but the Blitz went on until May 1941, even though it was clear that the Germans had lost their chance to invade England.

Then in June 1941 the Germans invaded Russia instead. For the British, the worst was over - for the time being.

The Blitz had been a terrible experience. Many people saw their loved ones die and their homes destroyed. But despite their suffering, the British people had shown themselves to be very brave and to be as tough as old leather.

Britain had survived to fight on.

WHAT'S A BANANA?

AND THE CUPBOARD WAS BARE ...

WOLF PACKS

Britain, in case you haven't noticed, is an island.
Everything Britain needs from outside has to come by
ship or aeroplane. Hitler set out to sink Britain's ships
and to starve her of vital supplies such as petrol, metal
and food.

In fact, on the very day war was declared, a German
submarine sank the British liner, Athenia, bound for
Canada. Soon British ships were being sunk in their
hundreds and many British sailors died.

The Battle of the Atlantic, the longest battle of World
War II, had started.

The biggest threat to British ships was German submarines, *Untersee Boote* - or U-Boats as they were called in English. The U-Boats hunted the stormy seas of the North Atlantic in groups known as 'wolf packs', seeking to cut Britain's vital supplies of food, metals and other raw materials from North America.

Sheep-dogs

At the start of the War Britain had the largest fleet of merchant ships in the world, but that wouldn't last long once the U-Boats got their teeth into them. Soon the merchant ships were organised into convoys for the voyage from America. Each convoy was protected by warships of the Royal Navy.

Convoys might be over a hundred ships long, stretching for miles and miles across the Ocean. The warships would sail in front and behind and along the sides, like sheep-dogs working a flock of sheep.

AND SITTING DUCKS

The warships did their best to keep the U-Boats at bay, but once U-Boats were in among the ships of a British convoy they could do a lot of damage.

One of the most unpleasant jobs of the War was to be a merchant sailor in the North Atlantic, chugging along in a large unarmed ship and knowing that U-Boats were lurking in the dark waters below.  Huge numbers of British ships were sunk and their sailors drowned or tossed in life-rafts in the icy sea.

But just enough supplies got through to keep Britain going ...

GROW YOUR OWN!

Due to the loss of so many supply-ships, if the British weren't very careful they might be starved into surrendering. So food was as important for the war effort as guns and bullets. The slogan of the day was '*Dig for Victory*!'.

 Vegetable patches were grown in public parks and private front gardens. Allotments spread across the land.

 Farmers grew more crops on their land with the help of extra workers.

Many households kept hens or a pig. There were 'pig clubs' for those who wanted part share of a pig.

NO, YOU CAN'T HAVE ANY MORE!

There was a better chance of eating a badger than a banana. Food and drink which could not be grown in Britain, such as oranges, tea and bananas, was soon in very short supply. Some people never saw a banana until the War was over.

The Government started a system of rationing, which guaranteed a small but equal quantity of some basic foods for everybody. In fact, poor people ate better in the War than they had before it started. In general people ate fewer meat and dairy products, and there were fewer heart attacks.

At the start, butter, sugar and bacon were rationed. Rations per person per week were:

> Butter 113 grams
> Sugar 793 grams
> Bacon 113 grams

Other foods were rationed later. Everyone had a ration book. They could save up 'points' and spend them all in one go if they wanted to.

The Germans had rationing too, although until towards the end of the War they were better fed than the British. One thing they had enough of was bread. You could often see people in Berlin parks trying to throw away stale bread without being noticed.

POWDERED EGG - YUM!

Most food was dull, and some of it was downright revolting. A lot of eggs were dried and powdered to stop them going bad. It's hard to meet anyone who lived during that time who has a kind word for powdered egg, even though the Government tried to convince them that it was delicious.

The Government suggested lots of different recipes:

> Carrot marmalade, to help you see in the dark during the black-out.
> Rosehip syrup - good for vitamin C.
> Cakes made with powdered egg.

ROAST EAGLE

Lots of people ate out on cheap food sold in canteens and elsewhere. This was mainly because so many women were working full-time for the war effort that they didn't have time to cook for their families in the traditional way. The handful of posh restaurants had to use their imagination to produce interesting food. A hotel in Scotland offered gulls' eggs, rooks, and once, 'Roast Eagle and Two Veg'.

MAKE DO AND MEND

It wasn't just food that was rationed. Rationing was brought in for clothes in 1941, and as the War went on, people's clothes got shabbier and shabbier as they became worn out.

HERS

JEWELLERY FROM BOTTLE TOPS.

MASCARA MADE FROM BURNT CORK.

Tip for making silk stockings last longer - wash in methylated spirits and store in an air-tight jar.

STOCKINGS WERE SO RARE THAT SOME WOMEN PUT TEA OR GRAVY BROWNING ON THEIR BARE LEGS AND PAINTED 'SEAMS' ON THEM.

'UTILITY' DRESS. UTILITY GOODS WERE WELL-DESIGNED.

ANY OLD BITS OF TORN PARACHUTE SILK WERE USED FOR UNDERWEAR AND OTHER LUXURY ITEMS.

His

TO SAVE CLOTH, LAWS LIMITED THE STYLE OF MEN'S CLOTHES.

ONLY SINGLE-BREASTED JACKETS WERE ALLOWED.

A LAW LIMITED THE NUMBER OF POCKETS ON MEN'S JACKETS.

A LAW LIMITED THE LENGTH OF MEN'S SHIRT-TAILS.

TURN-UPS ON MEN'S TROUSERS WERE ILLEGAL.

SOCKS WERE DARNED AGAIN AND AGAIN.

183

FUEL GRUEL

Without fuel, a tank or a battleship is little more than a useless lump of metal. Fuel was food and drink to the armed forces, and as such it was as important to the war effort as food itself. It was vital not to waste precious petrol on non-military uses. Government posters asked: *'Is your journey really necessary?'*. To start with, petrol rations were enough to allow two hundred miles' travel per month for every car, but later all private motoring was banned.

People such as doctors who needed their cars for work could combine business with pleasure. For instance, a doctor could go to the shops while out visiting one of his or her patients.

BLACK MARKET

If you had the money, you could nearly always get what you wanted - despite rationing. Crooks like me, known as 'spivs', sold scarce goods on the illegal 'black market'. The goods we sold on the black market were often either stolen from somewhere or had been sold illegally by a farmer or shopkeeper outside the rationing system. Prices on the black market were much higher than elsewhere.

WASTE NOT WANT NOT

There was a use for everything. If the Government could have found a use for old toilet paper it would have done so. This would have been difficult because there wasn't any toilet paper at that time - people used cut squares of newspaper.

Everything that could be recycled was recycled:

Paper was useful for cases for shells and for recycling.

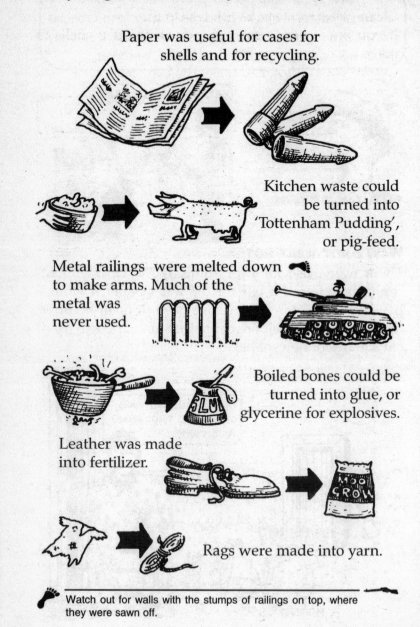

Kitchen waste could be turned into 'Tottenham Pudding', or pig-feed.

Metal railings were melted down to make arms. Much of the metal was never used.

Boiled bones could be turned into glue, or glycerine for explosives.

Leather was made into fertilizer.

Rags were made into yarn.

Watch out for walls with the stumps of railings on top, where they were sawn off.

Clean your woodwork with tea-dregs.
If you have some fresh eggs, crush the egg shells to make a scouring powder.
Cut up your old mac to make the baby's bib.

USEFUL TIPS NO 2 - AT SCHOOL

Write with thin, brittle pencils or a scratchy dip-in pen. Use your pencil down to the last two centimetres.

Use every bit of your exercise book, leave no margins and write all over the front and back covers.

BLIMMIN WIMMIN

WHAT GREAT-GRANDMA DID IN THE WAR.

> Millions of women took on jobs normally done by men. By the end of the War all fit women between eighteen and fifty-one had to work if they were asked to.

A LIST OF LIVELY LADIES

WOMEN WARRIORS

Women flocked to join the armed services. By the end of the War there were half a million in uniform. They did vital support work such as repairing aircraft and ships.

They were known by their initials:

WRNS, or *Wrens*, the Women's Royal Naval Service.
WAAFS, Women's Auxiliary Air Force.
ATS, Auxiliary Territorial Service.

FEMALE FARMERS

Most male farm labourers joined the army, so there weren't enough workers left on the farms. Food was desperately needed because of the Battle of the Atlantic. Enter the Women's Land Army.

Land girls had to work wherever they were sent, and they only got seven days' leave per year to go home. The work was often very tiring, especially if they came from a soft life in the city, but most of them were up to any challenge. Here are some typical Land Army jobs:

LAND GIRL

TREE FELLING

RAT CATCHING

POTATO PICKING

MILKING

HARVESTING

FACTORY FODDER

The munitions factories, which churned out tanks, guns and planes to replace those destroyed by the enemy, were mainly worked by women. Special nurseries were laid on so that women with children could work if a factory was near their home.

CLIPPIES
During the War, most bus-conductors were female.

CIVIL DEFENCE
Brave young women operated the floodlights to pick out enemy bombers. They also fired the anti-aircraft guns, although they weren't really meant to.

WVS
The Women's Voluntary Service helped out all over the place. They helped with evacuation, took food to bombed-out houses and greeted the survivors of Dunkirk.

While British women were expected to help with the war effort, before the War the Nazis discouraged German women from working. As already noted, German women were expected to stay at home and breed new members of the Master Race. It wasn't important whether they married or not - so long as they had children.

Real advertisement in a German newspaper:

```
Two vital, lusty, race-conscious
Brünhildes desirous of serving their
fatherland in the form most
ennobling women, would like to make
the acquaintance of two similarly-
inclined Siegfrieds. Marriage not of
essential importance.
```

However, once the War started, the Nazis realised that they needed more women to work in the factories because so many German men were in the army. But now they had the problem of convincing the women that they should work outside the home after all.

They weren't very successful.

And when the hours of factory work were lengthened, there was a big rise in the number of German women then in work who stayed at home sick.

FEATHERED FRIEND

This bird has joined the Royal Navy due to a misunderstanding. What kind of bird is it?

1. A Golden Eagle
2. A Buzzard
3. A Wren

Answer 3. A Wren of course - this meant WRNS or Women's Royal Naval Service.

WORKERS' PLAYTIME

HEE HEE AND HAW HAW.

WILLING WORKERS - AND NOT SO WILLING

The problem with war is that the other side keeps destroying all your tanks, ships and other gear. It's a hard job to keep up, let alone increase the amount of weapons for your forces to use. So factories are as important as armies - which is why the other side tries to bomb them, of course. Towards the end of the War there were five million people doing war work (which included working on the land), many of them women, all busy as ants in an antheap.

Thousands of small businesses turned their hands to producing war material. For instance some furniture makers made parts for an all-wood plane, the 'Wooden Wonder', otherwise known as the De Havilland Mosquito.

And hundreds of brand-new factories were built, some of them underground to avoid the bombs. Near Bath, 279,000 square metres of old stone-quarry became an underground aircraft factory.

Without fuel all the tanks and ships made in the factories would be useless, and without fuel the factories would have been useless as well. Fortunately, at the time of the Second World War many factories ran on coal, and Britain had enough coal for all its needs; the only problem was digging it out. This is why mining became a 'reserved occupation', meaning that miners weren't allowed to join the armed forces. Lots of conscientious objectors worked in the mines, and, towards the end of the War, many men who wanted to join the army had to go and work in the mines instead. It was that important.

As for the unwilling workers: prisoners of war also helped with the war effort. Apart from thousands of Italians, there were 400,000 German prisoners in Britain by the end of the War, 90,000 of them working on the land. Many chose to stay on after the War was over. One such, Bert Trautmann, became famous as the goalkeeper for Manchester City.

Things were different in Germany, where millions of workers from the conquered lands in Poland, Czechoslovakia and Russia were treated like slaves. They worked as little as they could get away with and would 'put a spanner in the works' if possible. But if they were caught, punishments for undermining the Nazi war effort were horrific, including beating and starvation.

What! No telly?

In a war, morale is very important. What this means is that if people are happy and believe they can win, they will work and fight much harder than if they are depressed and think they are going to lose.

So it was important to keep the workers happy. There was no television during the War and everyone listened to the wireless. Wireless was the best way to cheer them up.

Music While You Work was pumped into countless factories over their loud-speaker systems.

ITMA (*It's That Man Again*) was a very popular radio and television comedy.

Workers' Playtime was a lunchtime programme that came on three times a week in factory canteens, and was recorded in canteens around the country.

E-very N-ight S-omething A-wful

As well as radio programmes, the Government organised live shows. The original idea behind ENSA, the Entertainments National Service Association, was to cheer up the troops by putting on special travelling shows. There were ENSA performers with the army when it escaped from the Germans at Dunkirk. Later there were ENSA shows in factories as well. They performed in the canteens during lunch-breaks.

GOOSE-STEPS AND PROPER GANDERS

In a war, governments try to persuade their people that they are fighting for the right side and that their side is winning - even if it isn't. They make sure lots of encouraging news stories appear in the papers and on the television and radio. They also give out pamphlets and posters. All this stuff is called 'propaganda'.

British and American propaganda told people that the British side were kind and democratic, and that the Nazis were evil maniacs who shouted all the time and goose-stepped  around in jack-boots, trying to conquer the world - which was all true up to a point.

German propaganda told its people that their enemies were trying to destroy Europe and that the Germans, led by the Nazis, were trying to defend it - which wasn't really true at all.

HAW HAW

War-time governments mostly use propaganda to gee-up their own people, but they also use it to make the enemy population feel bad. The Nazis used to beam a

The *goose-step* is a style of marching where the leg is raised very high and straight in front.

radio programme into Britain, telling us how badly we were doing in the War.

They found an Irish Nazi called William Joyce who was willing to be their announcer. He was nick-named 'Lord Haw Haw' by the British press because he tried to talk with an upper-class English accent. (Try laughing in an upper-class way - 'haw, haw, haw'.) Sometimes Lord Haw Haw's propaganda was strangely accurate, such as when he reported the exact time that the church clock had stopped in one English village. At other times it sounded like the make-believe of a maniac, such as when he said that a British battleship had been 'hit in the kettles'.

Lord Haw Haw kept working till the end of the War. He made his last broadcast blind drunk in the ruins of Berlin, just before Germany surrendered. After the War he was tried for high treason in London and executed.

RESIST IF YOU DARE!

LIFE ON THE OTHER SIDE.

LET ME OUT!

Europeans didn't want to be ruled by the Germans and didn't like the Nazis lording it over them. They wanted to be able to speak and read freely and to come and go as they pleased.

Fat hope! The Nazis ruled Europe with an iron hand. If one of their soldiers was killed, they were likely to shoot several innocent citizens in cold blood as a *reprisal*. Sometimes hundreds of innocent people were rounded-up and shot. Most people kept their heads down and got on with their lives as best they could. They showed their anger

at the Germans by walking out of restaurants if a German entered and other such unfriendly acts.

Most people but not all. Some brave souls fought back. They were known as the 'Resistance'.

Secrecy was vital. The Resistance was organised in 'networks'. Each network stayed as separate as possible from other networks so that if one was betrayed the others would not be affected.

THE WORK OF A RESISTANCE AGENT

There was plenty of work for the Resistance to do:

Help Jews escape.

Help prisoners of war escape.

Blow up railway lines.

Blow up factories.

Resistance fighters were very brave. They risked betrayal at any time. There were always plenty of people who hated having a Resistance member living in their town or village. Such people feared German reprisal shootings more than they wanted freedom from German rule.

If a Resistance agent or a secret agent from Britain was caught, they could expect no mercy. The SS would torture their victims in order to get them to give away information about other agents or Resistance fighters.

The torture and questioning might go on for weeks. Then when it was over the prisoner would probably be shot or sent away to *Nacht und Nebel*, or 'night and fog' in English. This meant being sent off to a German concentration camp and almost certain death.

SWING STORY

There was resistance in Germany too. One small piece of resistance was the 'Swing Youth Movement' which was partly about non-Nazi fashion and partly about non-Nazi music. The Nazis hated the Swing Youth Movement because Swing youths liked jazz, which had been invented by black Americans.

The Swing boys wore English-style clothes with a rolled-up umbrella, and the girls wore lots of un-Nazi make-up. The typical Swing youth whistled English hit tunes all the time. When they met each other they gave the Nazi straight-arm salute, but instead of saying 'heil Hitler', they said 'heil Benny' after the American dance band leader, Benny Goodman.

It couldn't last. They were soon rounded-up and sent to concentration camps to be punished.

Rebel Armies

In France, Greece and Yugoslavia secret resistance armies sprang up. They set up camps in the wild hills and forests, ready to attack the Germans.

The French resistance army was called the *Maquis*, from the French word for the scrubby landscape where they hid. They were loyal to the 'Free French' government whose leader, General De Gaulle, was based in London. The *Maquis* was mainly made up of young men who

De Gaulle

fled into the mountains in Southern France to avoid being shipped off to work in German factories. They slept in caves or built themselves log cabins and sprang surprise raids on German troops. In the Battle of Vercors 3,500 *Maquisards* fought unsuccessfully against 20,000 Germans. Around seven hundred *Maquisards* died.

Collaborate if you don't dare!

The Germans ruled through their army and the *SS*, but they also made use of local police forces and local Nazi sympathizers. People who helped the Germans were known as 'collaborators'. Every occupied country had lots of them. In several countries it was the local police who rounded-up Jews to be sent to German concentration camps.

There were many collaborators in France. Three

thousand Frenchmen joined SS army divisions, and there were plenty of political parties which collaborated as well. Worst of all were the *Milice Francais*. They were a force of about ninety thousand men who wore black berets. They loved to crush the Resistance and to bully the Jews in their areas.

The SS and the Milice were desperate to stamp out all opposition to their rule. They knew that many people were working secretly to overthrow them ...

SPIES

CAN YOU KEEP A SECRET?

SOE WHAT?

'Special Operations Executive' agents were volunteers who were dropped behind enemy lines to work with the local Resistance to cause as much trouble to the enemy as possible.

You have to be a very brave person to be dropped on to an unknown field at night in an enemy country with nothing but an old suitcase of spare clothes and a false name.

During the War around one and a half thousand agents were dropped into France alone. If they were caught they were treated like spies, because they did not wear uniforms like proper soldiers. If captured, soldiers in uniform were made prisoners of war, but agents and spies, dressed in civilian clothes, were usually tortured and shot.

JUST SOE STORY

SOE agent, South African George Dessing, was dropped by parachute - right into the middle of an SS training camp! After giving Nazi salutes to the guards, he casually walked out without being stopped.

Later the Germans used another agent called Leonard Andringa, whom they had caught and terrified into helping them, to lure Dessing to a meeting in a café. But Dessing sensed that something was wrong. Again he casually walked out - right past Andringa's German guard.

Realising that he was useless now that the Germans knew who he was, Dessing decided to escape. It took him a year to cross occupied Europe to neutral Switzerland.

CLASSIFIED CLASSROOM

Before they set off, the SOE agents had special training.

How to hide secret messages in a rolled up cigarette - and smoke it if in trouble.

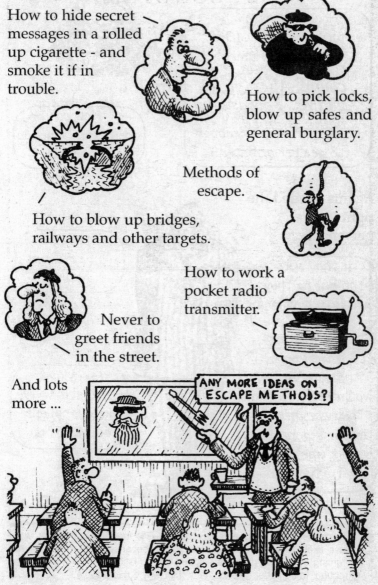

How to pick locks, blow up safes and general burglary.

Methods of escape.

How to blow up bridges, railways and other targets.

How to work a pocket radio transmitter.

Never to greet friends in the street.

And lots more ...

ANY MORE IDEAS ON ESCAPE METHODS?

RECIPE FOR A GOOD AGENT

Agents needed to know:

> How to behave in a foreign country. (One woman looked right when she wanted to cross the road, as if she were still in Britain where traffic drives on the left. It was enough to get her arrested.)

> How to speak the language fluently.

Agents needed the right kind of personality:

> They had to be good at acting.

> If they were too daring they wouldn't last long enough.

> If they were too careful they would stay alive but they wouldn't get anything done. SOE work was nearly always dangerous.

> They had to be able to live in a constant state of fear.

There were quite a lot of female agents. The theory was that they were less likely to be stopped by the police, because men who were not fighting or working might be stopped and questioned. Also women were thought to be better able to charm their way out of trouble.

The Drop

Sometimes agents were landed by boat on a lonely moonlit shore. More often they were taken to their destination by 'Lysander'.

The Lysander was a very special plane which was designed to drop agents and supplies into enemy territory. So as to be able to fly more than a thousand kilometres without refuelling, it had no guns or bombs or any extra weight. It could land in a field less than thirty-two metres long and take off again within just four minutes.

On the approach to their drop-point the pilots would swoop down to as low as 152 metres. Enemy searchlights were designed to aim high in the sky and they couldn't pick out low-flying planes.

All the pilot had to aim for might be a torch flashing in some bushes or a few small lights to mark out a landing field. Often they didn't even land, and they dropped their load, which might be an agent or supplies for the Resistance, by parachute.

Then the pilot flew back to England, but the poor old agent was alone in enemy territory - in the dark.

Agents were usually met by the local Resistance. But if things went wrong, they were on their own.

SIS

SOE agents weren't spies. Spies operated completely secretly and almost nobody knew who they were. One spy with access to reliable information, for instance on enemy troop movements, could be more valuable than a whole army of soldiers. So both sides lived in fear that enemy spies would give away their most secret decisions. British spies worked for the SIS, or Secret Intelligence Service (nowadays called MI6) which also tried to catch German spies.

Often the most useful information could be picked up by spies reading the newspapers or listening to conversations in the street. British government propaganda told people to be careful who they talked to in case a spy overheard them. Propaganda posters used slogans such as, *'careless talk costs lives', 'keep Mum - she's not so dumb'*.

I LEAVE FOR FRANCE ON FRIDAY.

SECRET CODES

Spies were useful, but code-breaking was even more useful. Most orders from the German Government to German troops and ships were sent by radio. It was easy to pick up the radio messages on radio masts in England. The problem was that they had all been turned into secret code on a machine like a typewriter, called *Enigma*.

1. Messages were scrambled up on an Enigma Machine.

SPUNGLE POODLEGLOTXXYW...

2. The scrambled messages were sent by radio.

3. The messages were fed into another Enigma Machine at the other end which had the same settings as the sending machine.

Unfortunately there were millions of different possible settings and the code was incredibly difficult to crack. But whoever cracked it would know what the Germans were planning, and where and when.

Fortunately the Poles had already worked out how Enigma worked and made a copy of the German machine.

Using the Polish information, the British set out to crack Enigma messages on a daily basis. They set up ULTRA (for Ultra-Secret), a special top-secret code-cracking operation, at Bletchley in Buckinghamshire. At its peak, more than ten thousand people worked there, including several brilliant mathematicians. The Germans never found out that ULTRA could read their secret Enigma messages.

I Spy

A German spy is listening to people talking in a café. He's not sure what all their words mean. Suppose you were a traitor - would you be able to help him?

1. A doodle-bug is ...
a.   A scribbled drawing
b.   A flying bomb
c.   An insect which sucks blood slowly

2. Lee Enfield is ...
a.   A famous cricketer
b.   An ace fighter-pilot
c.   A rifle

3. An evacuee is ...
a.   The result of a stomach complaint
b.   Someone who is moved away from their home to a less dangerous area
c.   A thermos flask

Answers
1 - b. 2 - c. 3 - b.

LET'S ALL JOIN IN

WELL IT IS A WORLD WAR!

HORSE-MEAT IN WINTER

FRIENDS NO.1
The Nazis believed that Russian Communism was part of a Jewish plot to weaken Germany and stop the Nazi plan for a German empire. So when Hitler signed an agreement with the powerful Russian leader, Joseph Stalin, in 1939, the German people were amazed - as were the Russians.

BUT NOT FOR LONG
By summer 1940 Hitler had started to worry that the Russians might decide to attack Germany from the east. Also the Battle of Britain was going badly. So he stopped his plans for invading Britain and attacked Russia in June 1941.

Stalin is Russian for 'steel'. His real name was *Iosif Vissarionovich Dzhugashvili*. No wonder he changed it!

212

FRIENDS NO.2

Now that Russia was fighting Germany, Britain and Russia became allies. The British papers called Joseph Stalin, the Russian leader, 'Uncle Joe', as if he were a kind, jolly uncle, although really Stalin was a brutal dictator.

THAT'LL TEACH YOU!

The German armies struck deep into Russian territory. The Russian army was weak: Stalin had shot around half his own generals out of fear that they would rebel against him.

STAINLESS STEEL TEETH

Stalin started to reorganise the Russian army. He chose new, younger generals. One of them had stainless steel false teeth, because his real teeth had been kicked out by Stalin's police.

GENERAL WINTER

The Germans were defeated by the Russian weather as much as by the Russian army. Heavy showers of rain began to fall after they had struck deep into Russian territory. The rain turned the sandy roads to mud. The German lorries and even their tanks got stuck in it. They had to wait again and again for the mud to dry. Their advance slowed to a crawl.

They reached within 15 km of Moscow, but when *General Winter*, as the Russians called it, started in December the Germans were really in trouble. Not only did they lack winter clothing, but their supplies ran short ...

Wine for the officers froze and broke the bottles.

Butter was so cold it had to be sawn off the block.

Meat had to be hacked from frozen horses using axes.

LENINGRAD

The greatest siege of the War took place in Russia. Leningrad, or St Petersburg as it's known today, was the second largest city in the country. Before it was freed in January 1944 it was besieged by the Germans for 890 days. One and a half million people died.

RATS IN SUMMER

Meanwhile, in an attempt to divide the Germans and take the heat off the Russians, the British and Allied armies were fighting in Greece and North Africa.

The Allies beat the Italians in North Africa, but when they advanced into Greece they were defeated by the Germans and had to retreat back to Africa again.

In the battles that followed two brilliant generals faced each other.

FIELD MARSHAL ROMMEL
(*The Desert Fox*)

FIELD MARSHAL
MONTGOMERY

DARING

MODEST

MILITARY GENIUS

BRILLIANT LEADER

CAUTIOUS AND CLEVER

Rommel took over command of the German army in North Africa in February 1941. He soon won a series of brilliant victories over the British and their allies. But then, led by Montgomery and with help from their allies, the British, or 'Desert Rats' as those in North Africa were known, started to win.

By May 1943 the British and recently-arrived Americans had driven Rommel's troops from Africa and they had started on the long, slow fight up Italy.

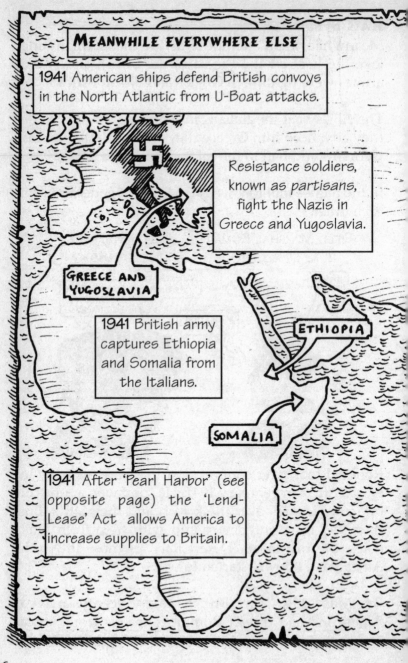

MEANWHILE EVERYWHERE ELSE

1941 American ships defend British convoys in the North Atlantic from U-Boat attacks.

Resistance soldiers, known as *partisans*, fight the Nazis in Greece and Yugoslavia.

GREECE AND YUGOSLAVIA

ETHIOPIA

1941 British army captures Ethiopia and Somalia from the Italians.

SOMALIA

1941 After 'Pearl Harbor' (see opposite page) the 'Lend-Lease' Act allows America to increase supplies to Britain.

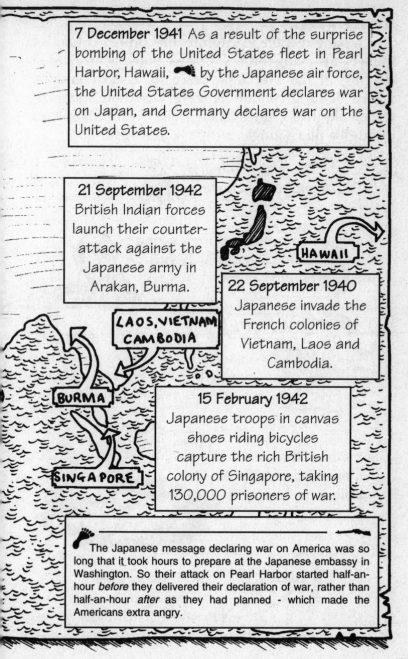

7 December 1941 As a result of the surprise bombing of the United States fleet in Pearl Harbor, Hawaii, 🐾 by the Japanese air force, the United States Government declares war on Japan, and Germany declares war on the United States.

21 September 1942 British Indian forces launch their counter-attack against the Japanese army in Arakan, Burma.

HAWAII

LAOS, VIETNAM CAMBODIA

22 September 1940 Japanese invade the French colonies of Vietnam, Laos and Cambodia.

BURMA

SINGAPORE

15 February 1942 Japanese troops in canvas shoes riding bicycles capture the rich British colony of Singapore, taking 130,000 prisoners of war.

🐾 The Japanese message declaring war on America was so long that it took hours to prepare at the Japanese embassy in Washington. So their attack on Pearl Harbor started half-an-hour *before* they delivered their declaration of war, rather than half-an-hour *after* as they had planned - which made the Americans extra angry.

217

JUNGLE FEVER

The Japanese tried to capture the British colony of India by attacking through Burma. Some of the fiercest fighting of the War took place in eastern jungles, where fighting conditions were incredibly tough. It could take five days to travel just twelve kilometres through a thorn jungle.

Fleas were a major problem in Burma.

Some of the troops in Burma weren't allowed to shave in case they cut themselves and caught typhus.

HELLO MATE

In Sri Lanka the deadly Russell's Viper used to snuggle up inside the soldiers' capes to keep out of the monsoon rain.

Sometimes they used elephants to carry their supplies.

MMM, LOVELY MUD

Mosquitoes were a problem almost everywhere. Their bites itched and they could cause malaria.

218

NAZIS AND NATIONALISTS

Not everyone in the British Empire and other countries outside Europe wanted to help the British. Some who were struggling for independence backed the Nazis.

CHANDRA BOSE

Large parts of India had been ruled by the British for over a hundred years. Most educated Indians wanted the British to leave, but did not want to use force to drive them out. However some Indians, like Subhas Chandra Bose, wanted to side with Germany and Japan. Bose became commander of the 'Indian National Army', supported by the Japanese.

RASCHID ALI

Iraq was controlled by the British at the start of the war. Raschid Ali was an Iraqi Prime Minister who backed an Arab rebellion against the British.

Luckily for the British however, the Nazis were so nasty that they managed to make enemies out of most people who might otherwise have been their friends.

SOLDIER'S CHOICE

Are you a northerner or a southerner?

You are colonel of a crack British paratroop regiment. Your regiment is trained to fight in some of the toughest country in the world.

You have a choice between two missions. Which do you choose?

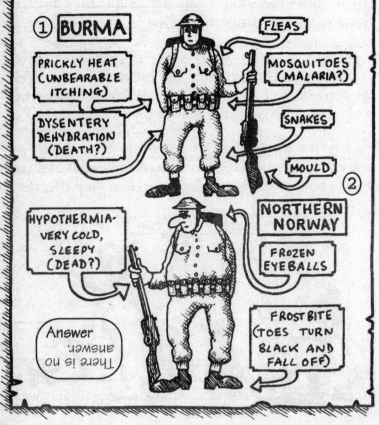

① **BURMA**

FLEAS

PRICKLY HEAT (UNBEARABLE ITCHING)

MOSQUITOES (MALARIA?)

DYSENTERY DEHYDRATION (DEATH?)

SNAKES

MOULD

②

HYPOTHERMIA- VERY COLD, SLEEPY (DEAD?)

NORTHERN NORWAY

FROZEN EYEBALLS

FROSTBITE (TOES TURN BLACK AND FALL OFF)

Answer

There is no answer.

220

BATTLESHIP BRITAIN

GETTING READY FOR THE OFF

BODY BUILDING

Immediately after their retreat from Dunkirk the British started on plans to invade Nazi-occupied Europe - just as soon as they and their allies were strong enough. By 1942 the Russians were asking them to hurry up and get on with it. An Allied invasion in the west would draw German forces away from their war with the Russians in the east.

Landing an army on an enemy shore is just about the hardest thing to do in wartime. Your troops will be mown down like skittles as they wade to shore. If your enemy army is the ruthless Nazi war machine you'll need a massive great army of your own to have any chance of success.

From 1941, men and machines poured into Britain from America and elsewhere. Before long Britain was bristling with guns like the quills on a porcupine, and there were enough men hidden in training camps in southern England to crush the German army just by sitting on it - if they could only get ashore in Europe.

WHERE YOU FROM THEN?
By spring 1944, 1,421,000 foreign troops had gathered in Britain. They came from all over the world.

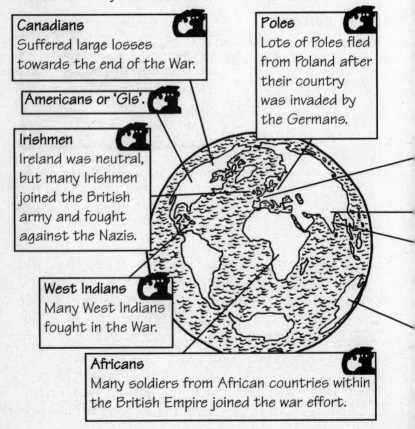

Canadians
Suffered large losses towards the end of the War.

Poles
Lots of Poles fled from Poland after their country was invaded by the Germans.

Americans or 'GIs'.

Irishmen
Ireland was neutral, but many Irishmen joined the British army and fought against the Nazis.

West Indians
Many West Indians fought in the War.

Africans
Many soldiers from African countries within the British Empire joined the war effort.

222

The largest group of foreign soldiers was the Americans, or 'GIs' as they were known from *Government Issue*, which was stamped on all their uniforms and other supplies.

I LOVE YOU, DARLING.

GIs were popular with English girls because they were paid three times as much as British soldiers, and they were very generous. They could get hold of luxuries such as cigarettes, nylon stockings and scented soap from their own Post Exchange stores and they knew the latest dance, called the jitterbug. By the end of the War at least sixty thousand English girls had become 'GI brides'.

Free French
Many Frenchmen and women fled German-occupied France. Known as the 'Free French' they fought the Nazis under the leadership of General De Gaulle.

Gurkhas
Gurkhas came from Nepal. There is still a Gurkha regiment in the British army today.

Indians
Hindu, Muslim and Sikh soldiers all fought against the Nazis.

An Australian

Australians and New Zealanders
The ANZACS, as they were known, fought bravely beside the British throughout the War.

223

A Handful of Heroes

The millions of men who fought in the armed forces of the Allies had some clever leaders. Here's a handful.

Dowding
Air Chief Marshal Sir Hugh 'Stuffy' Dowding was a brilliant leader of the RAF during the Battle of Britain. He was known as 'stuffy' because he lacked a sense of humour.

Eisenhower
General Dwight D. Eisenhower was the son of a poor Texan family. He was made Supreme Commander of the Allied invasion of Europe in 1944, and was so popular that in 1952 he was elected President of the USA.

Montgomery
Montgomery was a brilliant general who fought right through the War from Dunkirk to D-Day. He led the British army to victory in North Africa, before becoming commander of the British D-Day forces under Eisenhower.

Patton
General George Smith Patton was known as 'Old Blood-and-Guts' by his men. He was good at commanding fast-moving tanks and troops and led his 'Third Army' across France and into Germany in the summer of 1944.

For more information on D-Day, see page 230.

MEANWHILE - BACK IN BERLIN

NOT A NICE PLACE TO BE.

BOMBS AND MORE BOMBS

Apart from their powerful Japanese friends, and their not-so-powerful friends like Italy and Bulgaria, the Germans found themselves at war with most of the world. Life in Germany grew very tough. They had rationing and evacuations - and they had bombing.

Huge fleets of up to a thousand bombers set out from Britain to wreak destruction on German industries and cities. The British and their allies dropped millions of tons of bombs, killing many thousands of people during the War, and making more than seven million people homeless.

On 14 February 1945, in one of the worst air raids, 650,000 fire bombs were dropped on the city of Dresden, causing a fire-storm which ate up almost the entire city.

YELLOW STARS

If things were tough for ordinary German citizens, they were far tougher for those who did not belong to the Master Race. As early as 1941, all Jews were forced to wear a yellow star if they went out. They were rounded-up and sent to concentration camps in larger and larger numbers.

Then in 1942 the Nazis started their *Final Solution*. This was their plan to murder all the Jews they could get hold of. They built special gas chambers and furnaces in the concentration camps. More than six million Jews died.

In fact up to eleven million people may have been murdered during the Nazi *Holocaust* , not all in concentration camps. Victims included gypsies and disabled people among others, as well as Jews.

Holocaust means 'wholesale destruction'.

HIT-MEN FOR HITLER

Most Germans did not know about the Final Solution. It was not mentioned in the German newspapers or on the radio. However a handful of top officers realised that Hitler was leading his country to destruction, and they hatched several plans to kill him.

- *September 1938* - plan to capture Hitler alive and declare him insane (which shouldn't have been difficult!) failed because of poor leadership.

- *November 1939* - plot to kill Hitler failed because of hesitation by the plotters.

- *November 1939* - another plot to kill Hitler a few days later, this time with a push-button bomb. Hitler left early and the bomb killed seven other people.

- *March 1943* - plot to kill Hitler with a bomb hidden in a bottle of brandy on his private plane. The bomb failed to go off.

- *March 1943* - two bombs placed in Hitler's overcoat pockets, but he didn't wear the coat.

July 1944

THE CASE OF THE MOVING BRIEFCASE

Colonel Claus Philip Schenck Graf von Stauffenberg was as brave as his name was long, and he thought Hitler was pure evil. Being a high-ranking officer he was often at meetings when Hitler was present. At one such meeting he placed a bomb with a ten-minute delay in a briefcase and put the briefcase under the table near Hitler's chair. He then left the room. Unluckily another officer moved the briefcase out of the way to the other side of a wooden support. When the bomb exploded, Hitler was protected by the wooden support - and survived. Later Stauffenberg was arrested and shot.

This was the nearest anyone came to killing Hitler - except Hitler, who eventually committed suicide.

DOODLE-BUG AGAIN!

AND WORSE ...

The quickest way to get to Germany from Britain overland is to cross the English Channel from Dover to Calais and then drive like hell through Belgium. This is fine in peacetime, but not so easy if there's a massive great Nazi army waiting for you on the other side.

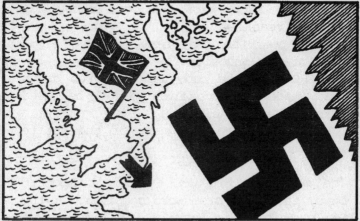

The British and their allies decided to land their armies in Normandy to the south of Calais, where German defences were slightly weaker than at Calais itself. The

229

day of the invasion was called 'D-Day' and it was planned for 6 June 1944. The American general Dwight D. Eisenhower was put in charge.

From early that morning the sky over southern England was dark with thousands upon thousands of planes on their way to France, and the ground thundered under the wheels of countless tanks and trucks as they made their way to transport ships in the southern ports. It was the largest water-borne invasion the world had ever seen.

CROSSWORD PUZZLE

In the weeks before D-Day a number of crossword clues appeared in the Daily Telegraph. The spy-catchers of MI6 became suspicious because the solutions to the clues were secret code names.

UTAH and OMAHA were the code names for landing beaches.
NEPTUNE was the code name for the naval side of the invasion.
MULBERRY was the code name for two giant ready-made harbours which were to be towed across the Channel.
OVERLORD was the code name of the entire invasion!

The men from MI6 went to visit Leonard Dawe, the chief crossword compiler for the Daily Telegraph. Luckily for him he was able to convince them that it was all a fantastic coincidence.

The German army was smaller than the Allies', but even so the invasion could have ended in disaster had the Germans fought back more quickly. But none of the top German commanders were available to order the German forces to start fighting back:

- No one dared to wake Hitler till late in the morning.

- Rommel, back from Africa and now the German commander of Channel defences, was on a day-trip to Ulm for his wife's birthday.

- The commander of the tank corps in the invasion area was on a trip to Belgium.

- Another key German commander was with his girlfriend.

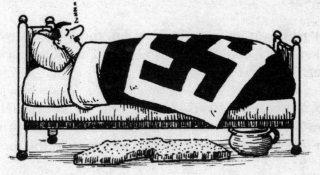

DOODLE-BUG AGAIN

Yes it's doodle-bug time again - where this book started. It was after the D-Day invasion that Hitler launched his doodle-bug flying bombs on London.

Once the Allied army had landed in Normandy it was only a matter of time before Germany was defeated. But Hitler refused to accept that he had lost the War. He boasted about a secret weapon which would turn defeat into victory. This secret weapon was the doodle-bug. On 13 June, just a week after the D-Day invasion, the first doodle-bug landed in England.

Doodle-bugs were hard to shoot down from a plane, except at close range when you might get caught in the blast. RAF pilots would fly alongside and tip a  wing beneath the doodle-bug so that it rolled out of control and crashed harmlessly.

Doodle-bugs killed six thousand people before the War was over.

Hitler had another secret weapon, the V2. This was a rocket which could fly at 5,793 kph. They killed nearly three thousand people.

The V weapons caused a second mass-evacuation from London, but they did nothing to break the British war effort. They were Hitler's last throw of the dice.

GOODBYE ADOLF

By April 1945 the Allies had fought their way to within a few kilometres of Hitler's Berlin headquarters, hidden in a vast concrete bunker in the centre of the city. Although defeat was staring him in the face, Hitler could not bring himself to accept that the War was lost. As if in a dream, he spent hours playing with models of the Nazi buildings he planned to build after the War was over.

Finally, when the roar of guns was almost crashing in his ears, he married his long-time mistress, Eva Braun, and at around 3.30 pm on 30 April 1945 they committed suicide together in the bunker. Next day top Nazi Goebbels and his wife poisoned their six children and then killed themselves as well.

THE HORRIBLE TRUTH

The War was as good as over. But as the victorious Allies spread out over conquered Germany they were horrified to find that the Nazi empire had been far nastier than they had imagined.

They discovered the concentration camps, which were full of of starving and dead victims.

Such crimes could not go unpunished. First of all it was planned that the entire German people should suffer by being stripped of all their industries and left to live like poor farmers, but this plan, the 'Morgenthau Plan', was soon thrown out - after all, not all Germans were Nazis.

It was the Nazi leaders who had whipped up hatred of the Jews and others and caused the War in the first place. So the Allies decided to punish the German leaders - those who were still alive anyway. Following this decision there were many local trials of war-criminals, but the biggest trial was held at Nuremberg, where twenty-one top Nazis were tried and twelve were sentenced to death.

LITTLE BOY AND FAT MAN

In fact the War wasn't completely over. It was still fizzling on in the Far East, where the Japanese kept on fighting. The Japanese leaders refused to surrender even though they were losing.

The Americans decided to end the War with one almighty blow. They had been working in secret on the very first atom bomb. On 6 August 1945 *Little Boy* exploded over the Japanese city of Hiroshima. Looking

back on the cloud of dust from the explosion which rose ten thousand metres into the air, one of the American airmen described it as *a peep into hell*. Around 270,000 people died as a result of that one explosion.

But still the Japanese leaders would not surrender.

So on 9 August *Fat Man* was dropped on the city of Nagasaki, killing a further 87,000 people. The Japanese leaders agreed to surrender soon afterwards.

Now the War really was over.

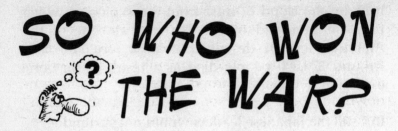

SO WHO WON THE WAR?

WELL SOMEONE MUST HAVE.

ON THE ROAD

When the War ended, Europe was a sad sight. Many towns had been destroyed by bombs and guns, their ruined buildings stood open to the wind and rain. On the roads more than twenty million refugees were on the move, some trying to return home, others simply moving to where they hoped they might be safe to rebuild their lives.

In the last stages of the war, the Russians had burst through the eastern defences of the once-mighty German army and had raced across Germany, at the same time as the Americans, the British and their allies had been advancing from the west. The Russians were half way across Germany when peace was declared.

And that's where the Russians stayed.

After the war was over, many of the homeless people on the roads of Europe were refugees trying to escape from the Russians, who now wanted to keep as many people as possible under their control, partly because they didn't trust the other Allies. As Churchill said later, it was as if an 'iron curtain' had been drawn across the middle of Europe. When the curtain came down, the poor people on the Russian side weren't even allowed to visit their relations on the other side.

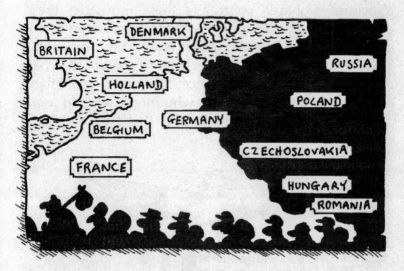

THE BIRTH OF THE BRUSSEL SPROUT

Meanwhile the Americans hatched up a scheme, called the 'Marshall Aid Plan', to lend more than a thousand million dollars to European countries, including Germany. This would help to feed the people and get industry running again.

Stalin refused Marshall Aid because of his distrust of the Americans, and life in the countries behind the Iron Curtain stayed tough for years and years. But gradually Western Europe started to grow rich and comfy again.

But would the European countries use their money to buy more guns so as to have another war in a few years time? After all, they'd had two massive great wars in just thirty-one years.

Then in May 1950 the French had a brilliant idea: new weapons could not be made without coal and steel, so if countries shared control of these industries they could not make weapons without permission from each other. War between them would be impossible. The French suggested a federation to control the coal and steel industries of France, Germany and other countries of western Europe who might wish to join. The Germans were all in favour; they too had had enough of wars.

Seven years later the Coal and Steel Federation became the famous Common Market, with its headquarters at Brussels in Belgium - one of the main reasons there has been no war in western Europe since World War II ended.

THE LION LICKS ITS WOUNDS

Meanwhile, Britain after the War was like a tired old lion that's just been in a very bad fight. She had wounds everywhere and her fur was falling out. In other words: there was still rationing (it finally stopped in 1954), nearly five million people who had been in the armed forces needed to find new work, and last but not least, the Bank of England was almost out of cash.

But on the other hand, in spite of the hardship and suffering caused by the War, some good things had come out of it:

By 1943, people were better fed than they had been in the 1930s. Rationing had meant fare shares for all (well sort of) whatever their class.

Ordinary people felt that it was they who had really won the War, and not the bungling upper classes.

Women had got a taste for work and independence.

WINNIE WIN-A-LOT - OR NOT

VE Day, 8 May 1945, or 'Victory in Europe Day' to give it its full title, was Winnie's proudest day. He was mobbed by happy, singing crowds of people in the streets of London while church-bells rang and the ships in the ports hooted their sirens.

But as things turned out, although Hitler hadn't won the War, neither had Winston Churchill. In the first general election after the War, in July 1945, poor old Winnie was voted out of office, and Clement Attlee, leader of the Labour Party, became Prime Minister.

People were grateful to Churchill for leading them to victory, but he was leader of the Tory Party. Many felt that the Tories wanted to lead Britain back to the bad old days before the War, when the upper classes ruled and the poor were meant to do as they were told. The Labour Party on the other hand, promised to help ordinary people.

'THINGS I WANT TO DO' BY CLEMENT ATTLEE, LABOUR PRIME MINISTER.

The 1945 Labour Government had big ideas on how Britain should change now the War was over. They wanted to make it a better place for ordinary people:

 Nationalise the railways, the ports, the coal mines and the gas and electricity industries.

Build lots of houses for homeless people.

 Start a National Health Service to provide free health care for everyone.

Make sure old age pensioners and unemployed people have enough money to live on.

If a government *nationalises* something, for instance an industry like the railways, this means the government has bought the industry, so it is now owned by the general public - the idea being that the government will run it for the good of the public not just the good of the former private owners.

WHAT WAS THE POINT OF IT ALL?

Many years have passed since the doodle-bugs fell on London. Great-Grandma and Great-Grandpa have grown old or died. The black-out curtains have long since mouldered away, and the only ration books and gas-masks you're likely to see are in museums. Just a few clues remain to remind us of that terrifying time.

 Clue No. 1 Many cities, like Coventry or Plymouth, have hardly any old buildings, because they were bombed to bits.

 Clue No. 2 We have a National Health Service and a Welfare State.

 Clue No. 3 The European Union has brought the countries of western Europe closer than they have ever been before.

 Clue No. 4 Perhaps the most important clue of all is the fact we don't live under Hitler's nightmare empire or Third Reich - the millions of people who died fighting the Nazis did not die in vain.

ANSWERS TO W.W.I QUIZ QUESTIONS

ORDER YOUR STARTERS, PAGE 26

1-bca. You can't demolish an entire country!
2-acb. Miners had nothing to do with it.
3-bca. A new moustache every day is impossible!

WAR FEVER, PAGE 35

1-b. In August 1914 the bombing hadn't started.
2-c. Britain had a small army and no conscription.
3-b. 'Conchie' meant 'conscientious objector'.
4-b. Aliens in Britain were sent to internment camps.

AIR SLIPS, PAGE 80

1. Parachutes weren't allowed until the end of the war.
2. Jet planes hadn't been invented yet.
3. Bombing of palaces was forbidden by the Kaiser.

A DOMESTIC SCENE, PAGE 96

By 1917, it was forbidden to feed bread to dogs in Britain.

FASHION VICTIM, PAGE 105

1. Long hair, long skirts and no make-up were normal before the War.
2. Shorter hair, shorter skirts, make-up and smoking in public became acceptable during the War.

WORLD WAR II SURVIVORS' GUIDE

All war is horrible. World War II was more horrible than most. Now that you've finished this book, find out how you would have got along if you had had to live through it.

1. Your train draws into a station. You want to know if you should get out. Do you ...

a. Ask someone?
b. Read the station sign?
c. Wait for the announcement?

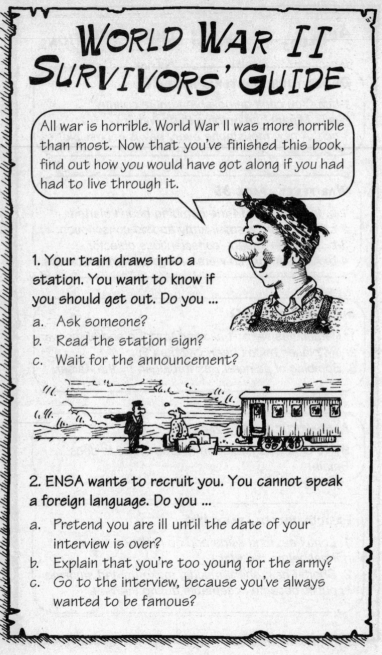

2. ENSA wants to recruit you. You cannot speak a foreign language. Do you ...

a. Pretend you are ill until the date of your interview is over?
b. Explain that you're too young for the army?
c. Go to the interview, because you've always wanted to be famous?

3. Your family has to visit a sick aunt but your petrol ration is all used up. A friend offers to sell you some, but it's a red colour. Do you ...

a. Refuse it because the petrol's probably gone off?
b. Take it anyway?
c. Refuse because it's illegal?

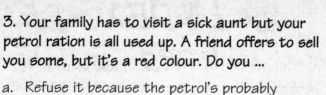

4. The air raid siren has started to wail. Your dog is frightened. Before you take shelter in your local air-raid shelter, do you ...

a. Make him comfortable in the cellar?
b. Let him out to find a safe place in the garden?
c. Take him with you?

Answers

1 - **a.** The guard may shout the name of the station, but it's safest to ask someone.

2 - **c.** ENSA is the Entertainments National Service Association. Members don't fight.

3 - **c.** The police dye some black-market petrol red so as to catch the people who use it.

4 - **a.** Dogs weren't allowed in the public air-raid shelters.

INDEX

NOW READ ON

Here are some books, in case you want to read about the two World Wars in more detail. You should be able to find them in your local library or bookshop.

WORLD WAR I
GROWING UP IN THE FIRST WORLD WAR
By Renée Huggett (Batsford 1985) Although the focus is on children, this book is about far more than that. It paints an excellent picture of what life was like at the time of the Great War, both in Britain and further afield. It has a great many excellent photos which help bring the subject to life.

THE LAST CZAR
By WHC Smith (Wayland 1973) Czar Nicholas II and all his family were murdered by the Bolsheviks in Russia in 1917 (see page 110), at the start of the Russian Revolution. That Revolution, born out of the horror of the First World War, lead to the Cold War which has dominated recent history. This book tells the story of what went wrong.

WORLD WAR II
WOMAN IN ARMS
By Russell Braddon (Armada 1989)
The true story of the amazing young Australian, Nancy Wake, who parachuted into German-occupied France in 1943 with a million francs and instructions to lead the French Resistance in her area.

THE SECRET WORLD WAR II
By Don Lawson (Franklin Watts 1978)
All about the allied spies who fought their dangerous
war in secret. Find out about secret codes and the work
of undercover agents behind enemy lines.

THE EVACUATION
By Bob Holman (Lion Publishing Plc. 1995)
Find out how to get rid of head lice and what life was
really like for town children living in the country for
the first time in their lives.

BATTLE OF THE ATLANTIC
By Kenneth Allen (Wayland 1973)
The true story of the grim, ghastly war between the
German U-boats and the brave sailors of the Atlantic
convoys.

ABOUT THE AUTHOR

Bob Fowke is a popular author of children's
books. With various friends and colleagues, he has
created many unusual and entertaining works on
all manner of subjects.

There's always more to his books than meets the
eye - look at all the entries in the index of this one!